ON FREE

OF THE WILL

The Library of Liberal Arts
OSKAR PIEST, FOUNDER

ON FREE CHOICE
OF THE WILL

SAINT AUGUSTINE

Translated by
ANNA S. BENJAMIN

and
L. H. HACKSTAFF

With an Introduction by
L. H. HACKSTAFF

THE BOBBS-MERRILL COMPANY, INC.
INDIANAPOLIS · NEW YORK

Saint Augustine: 354-430

THE BOBBS-MERRILL COMPANY, INC.

Printed in the United States of America

Library of Congress Catalog Card Number 63-16932

ISBN-0-672-60368-3 (pbk)

Eighth Printing

TRANSLATORS' PREFACE

We shall not follow the custom which dictates that translators' prefaces include, as a defense, an elaborate appeal to the impossibility of translating from one language to another. While the act of translation needs no defense, it does require a warning: discussing the translated text is interpreting an interpretation, not the original work. Translation makes available the translators' interpretation of an author and, like any form of reading and interpreting a text, contains distortion as the element inevitably introduced by the differences in era, society, personality, and intellect of the creator and reader. To minimize our distortion of the original work, we have tried to be consistent in the representation of the technical terms which Augustine uses, to preserve Augustine's method of presenting arguments in the negative, and to express the force of every word in its context. We hope that we may describe, at least in silhouette, that striking image of the author's mind: the style of the Augustinian sentence, replete with qualifiers and faithful to the tradition of Ciceronian Latin.

The text on which the translation is based is that edited by William M. Green, *Sancti Aureli Augustini opera: De libero arbitrio libri tres (corpus scriptorum ecclesiasticorum latinorum,* Volume LXXIV), Vienna, 1956. We have preserved the chapter divisions of this text; the marginal numbers correspond to its section numbers.

All notes are those of the translators. Scriptural attributions in these notes refer to the Douay Version of the Bible; the corresponding text in the Authorized Version is given in parentheses, when its location differs from that in the Douay. The biblical quotations themselves, however, are translated directly from Augustine's text.

A. S. B.
L. H. H.

CONTENTS

· · · · · · · · · · · · · · · ·

INTRODUCTION

The treatise *De libero arbitrio voluntatis* was begun by St. Augustine at Rome in the year 387–88, two years after his conversion to Catholic Christianity and one year after his baptism by St. Ambrose at Milan. It remained incomplete, however, until around 395. By this time, Augustine had returned to Africa, where he was ordained a priest of the Church at Hippo Regius. In 395 he returned to the treatise; Books Two and Three were "finished" [1] and added to the already completed manuscript of Book One. Some remarks on the composition of the treatise will be found at the end of this Introduction.

The work itself purports to be the product of discussions with friends carried on at Rome after the death of Augustine's mother, St. Monica, and before his return to Africa. While there is little need to question Augustine's assertion that the book "resulted" from these debates, it is clear that the treatise is no mere stenographic transcript. Indeed, one of the most interesting aspects of the work is to be found in its disclosure of Augustine's changing interests and emphases. Symptomatic of this is what may be called "the eclipse of Evodius." Even the most casual observer will note the manner in which Evodius, a vigorous interlocutor and lively objector in Book One, progressively becomes a mere auditor listening to the almost uninterrupted theological disquisitions of Augustine in Book Three. This "eclipse" corresponds to a gradual shift of emphasis in the material itself: Book One, though it is by no means devoid of theological concerns, is dominated by general philosophical issues, best expressed in the give and take of the semi-Platonic dialogue form. Book Three, on

---

[1] It is not clear from the evidence—internal or external—whether Augustine's "finishing" in 395 consisted in revising and editing an already existing manuscript brought from Italy, or in writing new material which he introduced as the second and third books of the treatise.

the other hand, concerns itself mainly with analysis of questions which may fairly be described as "theological," issues involving exposition and interpretation of the scriptural deposition.

The Background of the Treatise

In order to understand the place of *On Free Choice of the Will* in the development of Augustine's thought, it is necessary to understand the intellectual and spiritual ferment out of which it arose.

Augustine, born on November 13, 354, in Tagaste, a small agricultural town in North Africa, was the product of what we would now call a religiously mixed marriage. His father, Patricius, was a pagan; his mother, Monica, was a Christian. It was Monica's deepest concern that her son find his way into Catholic Christianity. Her hopes were not to be fulfilled, however, until her son had passed beyond his thirtieth year, although, as an unbaptized catechumen, Augustine remained within the fold of the North African Church until he was nineteen. His parents, though poor, provided their gifted and promising son with the finest education North Africa could offer; he studied the classical poets and orators at the excellent school at Madaura, mastering the niceties of Latin grammar and style. However, he neglected Greek, a deficiency in his education which had important consequences in later years; it left him the victim of Latin translations—often inaccurate or, worse, unavailable—of the Greek philosophical and theological documents which were crucial to his career as a Christian thinker.

At seventeen he journeyed to Carthage, where he soon became the outstanding student in the school of rhetoric. But the sumptuous and sensuous city accentuated another aspect of Augustine's being, an aspect whose origins he traces in his *Confessions* to his earliest youth. The life of Carthage made it plain that his bodily desires were as powerful as his mind was brilliant. He threw himself into the maelstrom of

Carthaginian indulgence, acquiring a mistress who bore him a son in his eighteenth year. Augustine piously named the infant Adeodatus, "given by God." He became increasingly addicted to the theater, in which, as he observed later, the images and shadows of life came to be more real for him than life itself.

For two years Augustine lived the life of Carthage, enjoying the expansiveness, sophistication, and freedom of the metropolis after the confinement of the outlying African towns in which he had grown up. But at the age of nineteen, he underwent the first of the successive conversions which were finally to bring him back to the religion of his upbringing, eventually transforming the brilliant young rhetorician into the saint of the *Confessions, The City of God, On the Trinity,* and the treatise *On Free Choice of the Will.*

In his nineteenth year—almost by accident—Augustine discovered philosophy. Any young man in the Roman world interested in persuasive speaking might reasonably be expected to study the rhetorical technique, language, and style of the master of Latin oratory, Marcus Tullius Cicero, and Augustine was no exception. While reading a philosophical essay by Cicero, the *Hortensius* (unfortunately no longer extant)[2] for the purpose of assimilating the techniques of the orator's eloquence, he found himself concentrating upon something quite other than he had intended: the ideas that Cicero's fine prose was designed to convey. For Augustine the essay occasioned one of the most stirring experiences of his

[2] Some scholars have argued that the *Hortensius* was a "close imitation" of Aristotle's *Protrepticus,* a hortatory work on the value of philosophy. The *Protrepticus* itself, however, like the *Hortensius,* was "lost"; but in the case of the *Protrepticus* a large number of fragments have survived—so many, in fact, that A.-H. Chroust, following I. Düring, has attempted a "reconstruction" now available in English (*Aristotle: Protrepticus, A Reconstruction,* Notre Dame, Indiana, 1964). If the *Hortensius* was a Latinized version of Aristotle's work, and if the Chroust–Düring reconstruction approximates the original, it is now possible for the general reader to survey something like the work that so stimulated the intellect of the young Augustine.

life; it constituted an exhortation to pass beyond rhetoric, oratory, the shows of the theater, and the superficiality of Carthaginian life.

> To Carthage then I came
> Burning burning burning burning [3]

Augustine came to Carthage burning with the fire of bodily lust; he left it thirteen years later, still burning, but now with the equally insatiable lust for truth and wisdom. Cicero's *Hortensius* was the immediate catalyst for this transformation. Augustine now sought truth with the same impatience, the same passion, the same immoderate yearning which he had formerly devoted to the life of the senses.

Having glimpsed the light of reason, Augustine began to reflect critically upon the religion of his upbringing, and to cast about for a religious or philosophical position which would satisfy the intellectual cravings aroused by the *Hortensius*. From his new perspective, orthodox Christianity seemed to leave much to be desired; instead of appealing to reason for its justification, it relied upon dogma and authority; to the young convert to philosophy, it seemed a religion of the superstitiously credulous man, not of the critically reflective one—and above all things Augustine yearned for the truth which the *Hortensius* had convinced him must be rational. In addition, the Christian Scriptures seemed remarkably naïve and dogmatic. Instead of providing clear-cut and intelligible answers to the religious and philosophical questions which now crowded in upon him from every side, the Scriptures, by the very simplicity of their statement, seemed only to obscure the issues; their answers succeeded merely in giving rise to more—and more difficult—questions.

The Scriptures suggest that God is omnibenevolent; what, then, is the source of suffering and sin? The scriptural answer is obscure. How can the eternal and infinite God be incarnated, become flesh, and be present in the body of a particular finite man? An astonishing claim; yet the scriptural answer

[3] T. S. Eliot, *The Waste Land,* III, 307–308.

is obscure. God put to trial? Scourged? Crucified like a common criminal? Astounding claims! Again the scriptural explanation is obscure.

These and innumerable other questions occurred, no doubt, to Augustine. His own commitment to Christianity had been naïve and environmental, and in recent years had become hardly even half-serious—ornamental, if anything, rather than functional. It was probably with a feeling of exhilarating emancipation that he turned from what must have seemed a childishly naïve faith, half believed, to the stimulating and autonomous quest for philosophic wisdom. Augustine's self-confidence and enthusiasm were, no doubt, magnified by his contact with his Christian contemporaries in Africa, most of whom were probably as unreflective about their beliefs as he had been previously. It is not difficult to imagine the acute young Augustine, skilled in the tricks of the rhetorical trade and now primed with at least a few of the rudimentary tools of the philosophic discipline, rapidly reducing his former Christian associates to the perplexing admission that they were holding incredible and paradoxical beliefs on the basis of the merest faith, a faith which their interlocutor would not have been slow to brand "pure superstition."

This phase of emancipation occasioned by the *Hortensius* forms a transitional period in Augustine's life. The search for wisdom involves, not only the negative critical examination of one's former views, but also the quest for the positive content of enlightenment and knowledge. Augustine did not accept the pagan eclecticism of Cicero. If he now rejected Catholic Christianity as unacceptable, there still remained a crucial spark of his former belief, surviving the mordant rationalism of his turn to philosophy. It may be argued that this survival, which Augustine himself would at this time have been hard put to rationalize in the Greek manner, constitutes the ideological focus which was to prevent him from reaching a personally satisfying philosophical equilibrium until his reconversion to Christianity in 386. The reason he offers for moving beyond the *Hortensius* is interesting, full of portents of the future: Augustine could find no mention of Christ in the works of Cicero—a fact not at all surprising, since the great orator died more than thirty years before Jesus' birth!

The enigmatic figure of Christ, imprinted upon Augustine's imagination since his infancy, would remain with him until his death—a mystery and a goad, a source of puzzlement, despair, and inspiration.

Instead of returning to the great systems of classical Greek thought—Platonism, Aristotelianism, Stoicism, Epicureanism, etc.—Augustine associated himself with one of the most vigorous opponents of Catholicism in North Africa: Manichaeism, the sect of Mani. This sect, often regarded as a Christian heresy, but having doctrinal and ethnic roots of its own, was founded by the Babylonian Mani in the mid-third century A.D. Little need be said about the life of Mani, since we are concerned here only with his central doctrine and its relation to the development of Augustine's thought. Suffice it to say that he preached successfully for a number of years, converting considerable numbers to his doctrine and mission; he was said to have received several special divine revelations and visitations, one of which disclosed to him that he was the Holy Ghost. Mani's remarkable claim was received about as cordially by the orthodox Zoroastrian priests as the parallel claim of Jesus was received by the high priests of Israel—and it was about as salubrious for Mani as for Jesus. He was officially executed—many authorities say crucified—in 277. But by bringing about the martyrdom of Mani, the Zoroastrians only gave added impetus to the new religion. The religion of the martyred "Holy Ghost" spread rapidly throughout the East. Twenty years after Mani's death, it had reached North Africa, and shortly thereafter had outposts throughout the remainder of the Roman Empire. Hence it was well established and well represented in Carthage when Augustine arrived.

Augustine informs us that after the Hortensian conversion, his thoughts were engaged by three central preoccupations:

the thirst for wisdom, a dissatisfaction with the Christian Scripture, and the love of the name of Christ. If the retrospective account of his state of mind given in the *Confessions* is accurate, we need not be puzzled by his attraction to Manichaeism. And in addition, Manichaeism provided what seemed to be an admirably plausible solution to a difficulty which appeared to Augustine insoluble on the premises of orthodox Christianity: the problem of evil.

We begin with the latter, since the solution to this problem is at the heart of Manichaean theology. In antiquity, the Epicureans had offered what they regarded as an irrefutable argument against religion. It holds against Christianity with greater force than against any pagan religion, since Christianity combines a doctrine of the radical contingency of all things upon God (the doctrine of creation *ex nihilo*) with the equally emphatic pronouncement of the omnibenevolence of Deity (the doctrine of the Divine Love). The Epicurean argument runs thus: Is God willing to prevent evil and suffering, but unable to do so? If so, He is impotent, or certainly not omnipotent. Is He able, but not willing? If so, He is malevolent, or certainly not omnibenevolent. Is He neither able nor willing? Then it is absurd to call Him God. Is He both willing and able? Then, whence comes evil?

Manichaeism constitutes an effort to take this argument seriously. Despite its many theoretical weaknesses, the position deserves to be considered with respect. In contrast with many Christian thinkers who either ignore the problem or dismiss it with patent sophisms or evasions, the Manichaeans attempted to deal with evil on its own terms. Orthodox Christianity triumphed over Manichaeism and Christian historians have, at times, dismissed this view as a completely eclectic and misbegotten position. If it is a distortion to say with A. A. Bevan [4] that Mani must be regarded as "a genius of the first order," it is equally false to suppose the Manichaean theory to be simply a patchwork of earlier religio-philosophical confessions totally devoid of genuine insight. It is a trib-

[4] *Encyclopedia of Religion and Ethics*, VIII, 400b.

ute to Augustine that he took the problem of evil seriously, refusing to commit himself to Christianity until he had seen his way to an acceptable solution to this problem. Put very briefly, the Manichaean position is: if evil exists, and if God is the cause of all existing things, then God is the cause of evil.

To place the Manichaean solution into perspective and to see it in contrast with the Christian resolution at which Augustine was arriving, it will be profitable to contrast it with some other positions:

1. *The ad maiorem gloriam Dei solution:* Evil was created in order to magnify, indeed to manifest, the glory of God. God permitted evil and sin in order to reveal his glory. If sinful man had not been created, God would never have had the occasion to show his compassion and justice. God would not have been able to disclose his magnificence, his equity, his power, or his mercy unless there had been sinners to be forgiven and sinners to be condemned. This is, of course, a little like saying that, if criminals did not exist, courts of justice would be compelled to create them in order to display their impartiality.

2. *The credo quia ad absurdum solution:* Evil is unintelligible. Its presence is a mystery, a divine obscurity. The only way to deal with the problem of evil is simply not to raise it. Believe in Christ and do not seek answers to unanswerable questions.

3. *The judicial solution:* Life on earth is a trial. Evil and suffering were created by God as a spur and a test for humanity. Upon man's response to the temptations of sin and the challenge of suffering depends man's trans-temporal destiny. Our temporal choices for good or evil determine our eternal recompense.

4. *The solution of eternal felicity:* This is almost always connected with the judicial solution. It accepts the full reality of evil and suffering, but maintains that for the man who has faith in God, shuns evildoing, and bears suffering with Christian patience, the sin and anguish of this world are

dwarfed to insignificance by the beatitude of eternal life in the presence of God. This popular solution is based upon the conception of compensation; but even in connection with the judicial solution, it fails to give a fully intelligible account of the issue. The notion of a trial is significant if, and only if, the outcome of the trial is at least theoretically in doubt, if the question of guilt or innocence is genuinely at issue. This necessary condition, however, is violated when the judge is omniscient, knowing in advance—indeed, from all eternity—the outcome of every case, whether it be vindication or condemnation.

5. *Evil regarded as an illusion:* Evil is "unreal"; the assumption that evil exists is false, based upon nothing more nor less than a mistaken subjective judgment. A position similar to this is to be found in ancient Stoicism and, in revised form, in modern Christian Science. The Stoics argued as follows: consider the judgment "I have been harmed." What does it mean? Only that certain quite objective events have taken place at some point in my life. These events do not present themselves equipped with labels stating severally, "I am a harmful event." No, on the contrary, it is I who, so to speak, paste such artificial labels on the quite neutral events in question. One has but to take away the opinion "I have been harmed" in order to remove the complaint. Remove the complaint "I have been harmed," and the harm is taken away. There is no evil in the world, unless we regard it so.

6. *The totality theory:* An interesting and sophisticated variant upon the illusion theory, attractive to Augustine and fully developed in the seventeenth century by Leibniz, might be entitled the "argument from the goodness of the totality." Like the Stoic variant, it attributes to ignorance or erroneous judgment the assertion that intrinsically evil events occur. This solution runs as follows: we judge certain events and/or experiences to be evil—and within the limitations of our purview we appear to be correct in so judging. But if we knew enough, if we could grasp the event, in all its relations, con-

nections, and consequences within the totality of all events, we would see that our judgment is incorrect, i.e., that the event in question makes a necessary and ineluctable contribution to the goodness, harmony, and beauty of the Whole. Just as, when one sits too close to the percussion instruments in an orchestra, they seem to produce little but irritating jangle and noise, although when heard in the proper perspective they make their own necessary contribution to the beauty of the symphony, so, according to the totality argument, evil is purely perspectival. Seen from the perspective of the Whole its contribution would be revealed, but seen from limited subjective perspectives, its value, its significance, and its very goodness are obscured. Perhaps the most celebrated application of the totality theory emerged in the Middle Ages in the doctrine of the *felix culpa*, the "fortunate Fall." Viewed from the perspective of Adam and his descendants, the fall from grace was a tragedy, a disaster— and so indeed it was. But seen from a larger perspective, the Fall takes on a new dimension; it becomes a blessing rather than a curse. For had Adam not sinned, there would have been no occasion for a blessing of literally incalculable significance. Were it not for the Fall, the world would not have known the gift of the Incarnation of God Himself in the life of Jesus, through whose passion and resurrection the disaster of the Fall was to be redeemed.

Like the other solutions, the totality theory makes certain assumptions, some of which verge upon begging the question. It is dangerous to specify what one would see *if* one knew enough, *if* one could see events in a larger (usually superhuman) perspective, *if* one grasped the Whole in all its connections and relations. These are indeed very speculative conditions. The objector whose view is less optimistic might suggest, like Schopenhauer or Nietzsche, that *if* one grasped the totality, one would see, not the totality argument's anthropomorphic best of all possible worlds, but a world so malignant that one's only recourse would be to cultivate a state of resignation or indifference to this totality, or else to devise a whole system of lies and self-deceptions about the world so as to make it tolerable. This view of the totality is as speculative as the first, but it serves to throw into high relief the implicit assumption, the *articula fidei* of the totality argument.

Manichaeism and Beyond

The Manichee would reject all of the above suggestions, regarding them as failing, in one way or another, to take evil seriously, or to deal successfully with the challenge set out by the Epicurean argument against religion (see p. xv). Solutions one through four of the problem of evil fail to absolve Deity from the charge of culpability for the existence of evil. Even if the good and the faithful are compensated for their suffering, this in no way exculpates God from the responsibility of creating, and/or sustaining, the conditions which require compensation, and if this is the case, the source of evil resides in the omnibenevolent God—a plain contradiction. Similarly, if an omnipotent and omniscient God could discover no more satisfactory means of exhibiting his excellence than the creation of misery, impotence, frustration, ignorance, and sin, it is difficult to understand what sense it makes to pay metaphysical compliments to him. How can the spectacle of such a world be rendered consistent with the claim of divine omnipotence? Again, solutions five and six constitute mere speculative evasions, refusals to regard the dark ground of existence with the seriousness it deserves. Both of these solutions involve an illegitimate selection from the evidence: the illusion and totality arguments implicitly emphasize the elements of harmony, unity, and orderly adaptation of means and ends in the universe, while they explain away or ignore the conflict, frustrations, injustice, and suffering which constitute a large part of the evidence to be taken into account. The Manichee would cheerfully admit that in some cases, perhaps even in many, moral evil (i.e., sin) and physical evil (i.e., suffering) are instrumental in the production of good. He would admit that the mar-

tyrdom of Socrates, of Jesus, of Mani—moral evils all—led to
the more vigorous dissemination of their doctrines and mis-
sions. He would cheerfully admit that the amputation of a
gangrenous leg, though painful, is instrumental to the preser-
vation of life and health. But he would seriously question the
statement that every moral and physical evil must necessarily
be instrumental to a greater good. To adopt this position is
to go beyond the evidence.

In an attempt to remain within the evidence and to treat
moral and physical evil with the seriousness it deserves, the
Manichee adopts a metaphysical dualism which he believes
to be in accord with the empirical facts. For nine years, despite deepening doubts, Augustine accepted this account of
evil. For nine years of critical reflection, Manichaean objections on this point—as on others to be considered below—
stood in the way of his return to Catholicism. The Manichaean solution states that there are two primal principles,
two substances, not just one: opposed to the benevolent
agency of the divine substance stands an irreconcilable and
conflicting principle of evil, equally eternal, equally ungen-
erated. This is the Manichaean dualism. With these two principles, Mani correlated two kingdoms: the Kingdom of Evil,
associated literally with darkness, and the Kingdom of Good,
associated literally with light. Here Manichaeism discloses its
debt to the religion of Zoroaster, and to other religions rep-
resenting the conflict of good and evil as a contest between
darkness and light (Ahriman, prince of darkness, and Ormazd,
prince of light, in Zoroastrianism). Ignoring the fantastic, fig-
urative, mythological, and eschatological elements with which
Mani embellished his theory, the Manichaean theory presents
the world of here and now as the locus of dramatic conflict
between the two primal principles. Evil, like good, has its
own integrity. Each is a substance expressing itself and ex-
foliating on the battleground of temporal existence. Man himself is ambivalent, embodying the conflict of the two principles. His being is inextricably bifocal. In the small, as
microcosm, man reproduces the grand conflict between good

and evil, light and darkness, which characterizes the universal macrocosm.

The world itself and man within it are a blend of incompatibles, products of the conflict of good and evil, the limited and the unlimited, the changeable and the transcendent, the darkness and the light. Man in his physical being is a product of Satan, but within him are confined portions of the eternal light. He is a discordant entity created in the image of the Dark, but compounded with Light. Sin and suffering originate from the Dark; virtue and beatitude from the Light. In a manner typical of the East and of the Platonic tradition of Greek philosophy, the forces of darkness in man were identified with the body and physical impulses, while the good was equated with the denial of the flesh and the exaltation of the spirit—although Mani considered the latter as not other than material. The task of the man who would achieve identification with the Light and salvation from the darkness of sin was to achieve the true knowledge of his real condition, making it possible for him to throw off the bonds of flesh which bind him to the Darkness. Manichaeism is thus a gnostic religion, one in which the final aim is to acquire knowledge of those truths which would deliver one from bondage. In contrast with Christianity, which demands the surrender of the will, and indeed of the whole man, to the Christ, the gnostic sects, of which Manichaeism is only one, emphasize the assent of the intellect to certain truths, acceptance of which is sufficient for deliverance. Thus the Manichaean dualism claims to do justice to the fact of evil in a way unavailable to the Christian, who is committed to account for the radical origination of all things from one primal source, the omnibenevolent God.

The Manichaean solution consists in taking the Epicurean trilemma by the horns. The horn Mani selects is that which assumes that the Deity is benevolent but *not* omnipotent. The god of the Manichee is indeed the source of all goodness, of all happiness, of all virtue—in short, of light; but the Light is, in principle, limited by the equally primordial Darkness

with which it is in conflict. Hence evil results from the very
limitation of the good.

The position is not only gnostic and dualistic, but also
rationalistic: the Manichee held that the saving gnosis or
knowledge which he professed to disclose acquired its justification, not through revelation or supernatural disclosure, but
through reason. This feature of the cult of Mani appealed
strongly to the philosophic disposition of the young Augustine. It spoke in the accents of the understanding and of
rational insight, not of faith and divine revelation, which it
scorned and attacked as superstition and irrationality. As a
"rational religion" it emphasized doctrine and ethics as opposed
to liturgy and ritual. The Manichees developed a form of
polemic against Christianity which bears some similarity to
the modern development known as the "higher criticism" of
the Bible. This technique consisted of isolating paradoxes and
contradictions in the Old Testament, statements which were
inconsistent with each other or with statements in the New
Testament. Again, this critical posture toward the Scriptures
corresponded with the attitude of Augustine at the time.
Finally, the figure of Christ appeared in the theory of the
Manichees as one of the great bringers of light. The occurrence of this figure in Manichaeism, though not emphasized
as in Catholic Christianity, satisfied for the time being that
central preoccupation described by Augustine as the "love of
the name of Christ."

As years passed, Augustine's initial enthusiasm for the
teachings of Mani waned. The obscurities of the doctrine,
which at first he thought to be a veil through which the
intellect could penetrate to discover the deep secrets behind,
seemed, after nine years of effort, to be meaningless obscur-
antism. No disclosure, no saving gnosis, no wisdom, no happiness could be found in this elaborate tangle of myth and
metaphysics. His readings from the works of the skeptics
threw doubt upon the whole Gnostic enterprise; what had
seemed potent with possibilities of disclosure now seemed like
so many fables. The Manichaean cult took great pride in the

knowledge it claimed concerning astronomy, particularly the wandering courses of the planets. Augustine discovered, through study of the work of others and by his own observations, that the astronomical calculations of his co-religionists were full of blunders. In astronomy their claim of gnosis gave every appearance of fraud. Doubts concerning the possibility of similar fraudulence in their claims to profounder gnosis, the gnosis that saves, inevitably suggested themselves. Thoroughly aroused by these and other difficulties in the doctrine of Mani, Augustine pressed his fellow Manichees for reply. They failed dismally, but promised that an expert was on the way, a certain Faustus, who would surely satisfy his doubts. Faustus came to Carthage in the winter of 382, but the great Manichaean authority likewise failed to meet the objections of the twenty-nine-year-old dialectician. He proved a modest and attractive man, but when pressed for answers to crucial questions, the gnosis was not in him. Disenchanted with Mani, yet still profoundly troubled by the moral, intellectual, and religious doubts and difficulties into which he had fallen, Augustine reluctantly underwent another conversion.

Having set Catholicism aside and having found no satisfaction in the religion of Mani, he came to wonder whether there was *any* truth available for human knowledge. Abandoning his former views, he embraced the doctrine of the Third Academy, the skeptical successor of Plato's school at Athens. Its founder and chief proponent was Carneades, who proposed a thoroughgoing and systematic skepticism: certain knowledge is not available to men; all things are subject to doubt; hence, the wise man gives assent to nothing at all, since if he should do so, he would inevitably fall into error, which of course is precisely what the wise man seeks to avoid. In the light of this wholesale confession of ignorance, the wise man must cling only to "probables" or "truth-like" statements which, while not affirmed to be true, serve as guiding principles for living.

Thus Augustine moved from the exhilarating affirmation

of truth and rationality, in the *Hortensius* period of 373, to the blank denial, in the early 380's, that truth is available to man and that any exertion of reason can bring about the ultimate disclosure. The Saint's adherence to skepticism did not persist beyond a few years. In the year 383, Augustine had moved from Carthage to Rome, and then to Milan in 384. This move was to be the most decisive in his life, for there Augustine came into contact with Ambrose, the Bishop of Milan. Two years later, profoundly influenced by the eloquence, reasonableness, and conviction of the Bishop, Augustine again became a catechumen in the Catholic Church, and in 387 received baptism at his hands.

By 388 work had begun on *De libero arbitrio*. This treatise, along with the other works in dialogue form which preceded it, shows with considerable clarity Augustine's path from Manichaeism to the Catholic faith. As pointed out earlier, one of the intellectual barriers that stood between Augustine and Christianity was the problem of evil. This is the central problem that gives unity to the present work. We have mentioned briefly the solution of the Manichees to which Augustine was early attracted. *De libero arbitrio* provides a fresh solution, one which is not only consistent with the faith of the Church, but which also avoids the insoluble dualism of the Manichees. The contention found here is essentially a Christianized version of that proposed by the adherents of Neo-Platonism; for the works of the Neo-Platonists formed the intellectual bridge between Augustine the pagan of 384 and Augustine the Christian of 387. The works of Plotinus and his followers, which Augustine studied assiduously in Latin translation, freed him of his doubts as to the conceivability of nonmaterial substance. They suggested a method of thoroughgoing self-examination, of introspection as the key to philosophic inquiry; through them he discovered the use of the "eye of the mind"—the study of one's own inner experience as the pathway to objective truth—a method which he never abandoned and which provided him with a means of escape from skepticism. They made clear to him that the problem of evil could be solved without having to recognize the existence of a positive, diabolical principle co-eternal with God. The Neo-Platonic alternative to Manichaean dualism is this: evil is not a substance, as the Manichees declare. It is not a positive reality in its own right, but rather a *privation* of reality, a defect in substance. All things are good insofar as they exist; to be is to be good.

But what then is evil? Has it no reality whatsoever? The answer to this question, from the viewpoint of Augustine's Christianized Neo-Platonism, is a qualified "yes" and a qualified "no." Insofar as one means by "reality" existence *qua* substance, evil has no reality, for it is *not* a substance. Apart from the good, it would not exist. If, however, one means by "reality" existence *qua* deficiency or imperfection in substances, evil exists, insofar as there are entities which lack perfection. There should be no misunderstanding here. Augustine maintains that all existing things are good—in that they exist. Evil stems not from their existence per se, but from their deficient *manner* of existence. They fail to attain perfection of their kind; evil, then, consists of the corruption of their goodness. Evil in man arises not from some evil principle embodied in his nature, but from the will's *free determination* to turn from higher things to lower, from eternal to temporal; to bind itself to things which, though good in themselves, lack the worth and dignity proper to itself. Thus evil is to be found in man's free choice to pervert and corrupt his own will by turning aside from that good which is proper to it, the ultimate good that is God. In this is found the core of Augustine's answer to the Manichees, and the center of his theodicy.

Every good is from God. Evil stems from the will's free choice to depart from its true vocation. This departure, this turning away, constitute the very nature of corruption and imperfection. Hence evil is to be explained, not as the creation of an incompetent God, not as the handiwork of some diabolic nature or principle, but as a result of the abuse of one of God's gifts, free will—an abuse which is to be attributed not to the Giver, but to those to whom it is given. This solution is undeniably dependent upon the theories of the Neo-Platonists; but its emphasis upon the will's radical responsibility, so often underlined in the present work, indicates that we are in the presence of an Augustine who is not merely another Neo-Platonist, but a Christian.

In concluding this section, it would be well to note that, unlike a number of later works of Augustine directed explicitly against Manichaeism, *De libero arbitrio* is not motivated solely by the polemic aim of refuting the heresy and of defending the Church against it. It is clear that when the discussions took place and Augustine began to write the treatise, his primary concern was to elucidate the difficulties of the problem of evil; to make clear the coherence and adequacy of the alternative solution he proposed; and to gain understanding in his own mind of the truths received by faith, by means of showing that those received truths offer or suggest solutions fully satisfying to reason. Indicative of the exploratory and, to a degree, tentative character of sections of the work are the occasions throughout the book in which Augustine raises and discusses issues for which, as it turns out, he is able to formulate no satisfactory or decisive answer, e.g., the interesting discussion of the alternative theories concerning the origin of the human soul. In this respect, the treatise resembles the earlier, more discursive and exploratory dialogues of the period of retreat at Cassiciacum prior to his baptism. Yet in other respects, the work anticipates, particularly in Book Three, with the almost complete eclipse of Evodius, the theological methods of the later Augustine. Even if the *Retractations* did not provide us with first-hand evidence of its sequential development, the differences of style and emphasis would have suggested such a developmental theory.

The Significance of the Book

As J. H. S. Burleigh has remarked in his recent study,[5] we find in Augustine's *De libero arbitrio* "a work which is the highwater mark of his philosophical writing." Certainly Augustine continued to regard it highly as a medium for the expression of his ideas. In a letter of 415 directed to Jerome, he states that the treatise has been widely circulated and that "many" are still possessed of the work.[6] In 405 he recommended it to the Manichee Secundinus as an effective presentation of his answer to the Manichaean heresy.[7] Likewise, when later Pelagian heretics tried to "adopt" the book, claiming that its position on human freedom is inconsistent with Augustine's more fully developed view of grace, he stoutly defended it, not only as consonant with the later doctrine, but as containing statements which explicitly anticipate his polemic against the followers of Pelagius (see Appendix, p. 158). There is no doubt, then, that Augustine and his associates considered the work of great importance.

De libero arbitrio, along with the earlier *De ordine,* offers the perceptive reader an impressive documentation of the profound influence of the later Platonism upon the developing doctrinal foundations of patristic Christianity. Indeed, it is not too great an exaggeration to say that Neo-Platonism provided Augustine and the Christian Platonists who followed him with the theoretical substructure on which their theology was built. It seems that Augustine never abandoned the Platonistic matrix of his Christian theology; but this powerful influence manifests itself more clearly in the present work than in any other extended work by the author. Perhaps this contention is best borne out with respect to the theory of hierarchical order which pervades the treatise. Reality is conceived in the manner of Plotinus, as a hierarchical

[5] *The City of God* (London, 1949), p. 72.
[6] Augustine, *Epistolae* 166. 7.
[7] *Contra Secundinum* 11.

order: at the upper extreme is the eternal reality of God; temporal, material things, the objects of the senses, occupy the lower extreme; between the extremes are found the various gradations and orders of spirituality, one of which is the order exemplified by the human soul. This Neo-Platonic framework should be kept clearly in mind in consideration of the occurrence of the term *ordinatus* (ordered) and the treatise's central doctrinal contention that sin and evil stem from the will's voluntary choice of the temporal goods of the body, as opposed to the eternal good epitomized by God.

The book is especially noteworthy in that it sets out in greater detail than any of Augustine's other works, large or small, his major argument for the existence of God: the argument to eternal truth. A large portion of Book Two is given over to the exposition of this argument, which is based upon the evidence of reason alone, making no appeal to revelation or authority. The proof is thoroughly Platonistic; it is grounded in the possibility of grasping eternal truth, truth whose warrant lies quite beyond the fabrications of the senses and of the mind, e.g., the truths of mathematics. It is contended that if such truths are granted, then this is sufficient to show the reality of a source of these truths, which is superior to the mind, i.e., the reality of Truth itself; either this is God, or if there be any being superior to Eternal Truth, then such a being is God. Nothing shows more clearly the Platonistic background of Augustine's theology than this proof.

In 429, Augustine wrote as follows concerning his efforts against the Manichees:

> I presented my arguments against these men in my book on free will: thus they suppose they are justified in complaining against me. Since it was impossible to bring up the authority of Sacred Writ in opposition to such perversion, I could not hope to present a completely decisive answer to these most difficult issues which arose, since I feared that the length of the work would be too great. By means of irrefutable argumentation (which I actually accomplished without direct appeal to the truth of any part

of the Holy Writ) I showed that God should be praised for all things, and that there are no grounds at all for their belief that there exists two co-eternal natures, one good, one evil, which co-exist together.[8]

Though the Saint seems almost to apologize for the paucity of scriptural exposition, exegesis, and derivation in *De libero arbitrio,* there is a sense in which the method Augustine uses here, for better or for worse, is more appealing in our own time than are the doctrinal treatises of later years with their wealth, indeed, their plethora of scriptural exegesis and their concentration upon polemic and doctrinal definition. *De libero arbitrio* is no substitute for the intensity and insight of the *Confessions;* it is no substitute for the subtlety, scope, and definition of *De trinitate;* but it may very well be argued that neither of these, nor any other of his works, better illustrates Augustine the philosopher, the Christian Platonist, the original thinker, the seeker after wisdom, than *De libero arbitrio.*

L. H. HACKSTAFF

[8] Augustine, *De dono perseverantiae* 6.

SELECTED BIBLIOGRAPHY

Works by Augustine

The City of God.

The Confessions.

Early dialogues: *De beata vita, Contra academicos, De ordine, Soliloquia* (contained in Volume I, *The Fathers of the Church*, New York, 1948).

On the Trinity.

An Augustine Synthesis, edited and compiled by Erich Przywara. New York, 1936.

Works on Augustine and his Time

BATTENHOUSE, R. W., ed. *Companion to the Study of St. Augustine.* New York, 1939.

BOURKE, E. J. *Augustine's Quest of Wisdom.* Milwaukee, 1945.

BURLEIGH, J. H. S. *The City of God.* London, 1949.

CHROUST, ANTON-HERMANN. *Aristotle: Protrepticus, A Reconstruction.* Notre Dame, Indiana, 1964.

COCHRANE, C. N. *Christianity and Classical Culture.* London, 1940.

D'ARCY, M. C., ed. *A Monument to St. Augustine.* London, 1930.

GILSON, E. *Introduction à l'étude de Saint Augustine.* 3rd ed., Paris, 1949.

POPE, HUGH. *St. Augustine of Hippo.* Baltimore, 1949.

SIMPSON, W. J. SPARROW. *St. Augustine's Conversion.* New York, 1930.

ON FREE CHOICE
OF THE WILL

BOOK ONE

I.
Is God the cause of evil?

Evodius.　　　Tell me, please, whether God is not the cause　1
of evil.

Augustine.　　　I shall, if you will explain what kind of evil
you mean. For we usually speak of evil in two senses: one
when we mean that someone has done evil; the other, when
we mean that someone has suffered evil.

E.　　　I want to know about both kinds.

A.　　　But if you know or believe that God is good (and it
is not right to believe otherwise), God does not do evil. Also,
if we admit that God is just (and it is sacrilege to deny this),
He assigns rewards to the righteous and punishments to the
wicked—punishments that are indeed evil for those who suffer
them. Therefore, if no one suffers punishment unjustly (this　2
too we must believe, since we believe that the universe is
governed by divine Providence), God is the cause of the second kind of evil, but not of the first.

E.　　　Then is there some other cause of the latter kind of
evil, which, as we found, God did not cause?

A.　　　Certainly, for evil could not have come into being　3
without a cause. However, if you ask what the cause may be,
I cannot say, since there is no one cause; rather, each evil man
is the cause of his own evildoing. If you doubt this, then
listen to what we said above: evil deeds are punished by the
justice of God. It would not be just to punish evil deeds if
they were not done willfully.

E.　　　I do not know whether anyone sins who has not　4
learned how to sin; but if this is the case, from whom, I ask,
have we learned how to sin?

A.　　　Do you think that education is something good?

3

E.   Who would dare to say that education is evil?

A.   Suppose it is neither good nor evil?

E.   I think it is good.

A.   Very well, provided that knowledge is given or awakened by education, and no one can learn anything except through education. Or do you disagree?

E.   I think that only good things can be learned through education.

5   *A.*   Therefore you must see that evil is not learned! Indeed, the very word "education" [*disciplina*] is derived from the verb "to learn" [*discere*].

E.   How is it then that man does evil, if evil is not learned?

A.   Perhaps because he avoids and turns from education, by which I mean the act of learning. But whether this or something else is true, the following is clear: since education is good and "education" is derived from "learning," evil can-
6   not be learned. For if evil is learned, then evil is a part of education and education will not be something good. However, as you yourself grant, it is good. Therefore evil is not learned and it is useless to ask from whom we learn evil. Or, if we learn evil, we learn so as to avoid it, not do it. From this reasoning we may say that to do evil is to turn from education.

7   *E.*   To proceed then, I think that there are two kinds of education: one by which we learn to do good, and another by which we learn to do evil. When you asked whether education was good, my attention was caught by the love of the good and I thought only of the education which has to do with good deeds. This is why I answered that education was good. Now, however, I realize that there is another kind of education which I assert without doubt is evil, and I now ask for the cause of this.

8   *A.*   At least you think that understanding is good?

E.   Yes, I think it so good that I do not see anything in man that could be more excellent, and I assert that there is no kind of understanding which can be evil.

A.   What then of this: if someone is taught and yet does 9
not understand, do you think he can be called a learned man?

E.   Absolutely not.

A.   If, therefore, every kind of understanding is good
and no one learns who does not understand, then everyone
who learns is doing good. For everyone who learns, understands; and everyone who understands is doing good. Therefore, whoever seeks the cause of our learning something is
surely asking for the cause of our doing good. So stop trying
to find some unknown evil teacher. If he is evil, he is not a
teacher; if he is a teacher, he is not evil.

II.
What must be believed about God.

E.   Since you force me to acknowledge that we do not 10
learn to do evil, then tell me why we do indeed do evil.

A.   You propose a question which disturbed me exceed-
ingly when I was still a youth, one which wearied me and
drove me into heresy,[1] and indeed caused my downfall. So
hurt was I by this fall, and so buried in a heap of empty
myths, that, had my love for discovering the truth not won
me divine aid, I could not have arisen from my fall, or re-
covered my breath so as to use even my previous right to
inquire after truth. And since my case was so zealously argued 11
that I was acquitted in this trial, I will follow with you the
very arguments by which I escaped. For God will aid us and
will make us understand what we believe. This is the course
prescribed by the prophet who says, "Unless you believe, you
shall not understand," [2] and we are aware that we consider
this course good for us. We believe, moreover, that everything
that exists is from God and yet that God is not the cause of
sins. Yet it perplexes the mind how God should not be indi-
rectly responsible for these sins, if they come from those very

[1] That is, Manichaeism.
[2] Is. 7:9, Septuagint.

souls that God created and if, moreover, these souls are from God.

12   *E.*   Now you have plainly stated the very thing which tortures my thought and which has impelled me to ask my question.

A.   Be of brave spirit and believe what you believe, for there is nothing worthier of belief, even though the reason why it is true may lie hidden. For to hold God supreme is most truly the beginning of piety; and no one holds Him supreme who does not believe Him to be omnipotent and absolutely changeless, Creator of all good things which He Himself transcends in excellence, and the most just Ruler, as well, of all that He has created. And He has not, like one who is not sufficient unto himself, been aided by any nature
13 in His creation. From this it follows that He created everything from nothing. From Himself He did not create Himself; rather He begot what was equal to Himself, whom we call the only Son of God. When we try to describe the Son of God more clearly we name Him the Power of God and the Wisdom of God, through which God made everything that was made from nothing. With this belief as our foundation, let us thus strive, with God's aid, toward an understanding of the question you have proposed.

III.
Lust is the source of evil.

14   *A.*   You are really asking why we do evil. But first we must discuss what evildoing is. Explain what your opinion is in this matter; if you cannot answer the whole of the question in a few brief words, at least make your views known to me by mentioning particular evil deeds.

E.   Adultery, homicide, sacrilege, not to mention others which time and memory do not permit me to recount. Who does not consider these evil?

15   *A.*   Then first tell me why you think adultery is an evil. Because the law forbids it?

E.   Certainly it is not an evil because the law forbids it.
Rather, adultery is forbidden because it is evil.

A.   What if someone should harass us by exalting the
delights of adultery, asking us why we condemn adultery as
evil and worthy of punishment? You do not suppose, do you,
that men who are eager not only to believe but even to understand ought to take refuge in the authority of law as a reason?   16
Indeed, I believe as you believe, and am firm in my belief; I
cry out that all people and nations ought to believe adultery
is evil. But now we are struggling to know with our understanding and to establish most firmly what we have already
accepted by faith. Therefore, consider as best you can and
tell me the reason why you know adultery to be wrong.

E.   I know that adultery is an evil because I myself
would be unwilling to allow adultery in the case of my wife.
And whoever does to another what he does not wish done
to himself, does evil.

A.   What if someone's lust is so great that he offers his   17
own wife to another and willingly allows her to be seduced
by the man with whose wife he in turn wants to have equal
license? Don't you think that he does evil?

E.   Yes, the worst evil!

A.   By the rule you mentioned such a man does not sin,
for he does nothing that he would not endure. You must find
some other reason by which to prove that adultery is evil.

E.   I think it is evil because I have often seen men con-   18
demned for this crime.

A.   What! Haven't you seen many men condemned for
just deeds? You need only to look back over history, that very
history (to avoid sending you to other books) which excels because of its divine authority: you will soon find there what
bad opinions we would have of the Apostles and all the
martyrs, if we decided that condemnation is a sure proof of
evildoing. All of these were judged worthy of condemnation
because of their confession of faith. Therefore, if evil is what-   19
ever is condemned, in those days it was evil to believe in
Christ and to confess the faith. If, on the other hand, not

everything that is condemned is evil, you must find another
reason for asserting that adultery is evil.

E.   I have no answer to give you.

20   A.   Perhaps then lust [*libido*] is the evil element in
adultery. As long as you look for evil in the overt act itself,
which can be seen, you are in difficulty. To help you to understand that the evil element in adultery is lust, consider the
case of a man who does not have the opportunity to lie with
another's wife; but nevertheless, if it is somehow obvious that
he would like to do so and would do so had he the opportunity, he is no less guilty than the man taken in the very
act.

21   E.   Nothing is more obvious, and I now see that there
is no need for a long discussion to show me how homicide
and sacrilege and all the other sins are evil. Now it is clear
that lust is dominant in every kind of evildoing.

IV.
What of certain crimes committed out of fear? What is an evil desire?

22   A.   Do you know that lust [*libido*] is also called desire
[*cupiditas*]?

E.   Yes.

A.   Do you, or do you not, think that there is any difference between desire and fear?

E.   I think that these are very different indeed.

A.   I imagine that you think so for this reason: desire
seeks, while fear avoids [its object].

E.   That is just it.

A.   Suppose someone kills a man, not through desire of
getting something, but through fear of suffering evil? He will
not be a murderer, will he?

23   E.   Yes, he will, for in that case it does not follow that
the deed is free from the motive of desire, since the man who
kills through fear desires to live without fear.

A.   Do you think that life without fear is a small good?

E. Life without fear is a great good, but it cannot come to the murderer through his crime.

A. I am not asking about what may come to him, but 24 rather about what he desires. Anyone who desires a life free of fear surely desires something good. Therefore, this desire is not blameworthy; otherwise we would blame all lovers of good. So we are forced to admit that there exist cases of murder in which the dominant factor of evil desire cannot be found. It will be false, then, to say that in all sins it is the domination of lust that makes evil; otherwise there will exist a kind of murder that cannot be a sin.

E. If to murder means to kill a man, murder can occur 25 sometimes without sin. For when the soldier kills an enemy or the judge or official puts a criminal to death, or when, by chance, a man unwillingly or unwisely lets a weapon escape from his hand, I do not think that these men sin when they slay a man.

A. I agree. Yet these men are not usually called murderers. Answer this, then: Do you think that the man who kills a master from whom he fears severe tortures is to be considered one of these men who, although they have killed, do not deserve the name of murderer?

E. I see that this is quite a different case. For the former man acts either according to the law or not contrary to the law; while the crime of the man who slays his master because of his fear of punishment is not approved by any law.

A. Again you bring me back to authority. But you must 26 remember that we have undertaken this study now so as to understand what we believe in. We do believe in laws, so we must try somehow, if we can, to understand the following question: May not the law which punishes this deed punish it wrongly?

E. The law is not at all wrong to punish the man who 27 willfully and knowingly murders his master. None of the others in our examples did that.

A. Come, do you remember that a little while ago you said that in every evil deed lust was the dominant factor, and that a deed is evil because of lust?

E.   Yes, I do remember.

28   *A.*   What! Have you not admitted, as well, that the man who desires to live without fear does not have an evil desire?

E.   I remember that too.

A.   Therefore, when a master is killed by a slave because of the slave's desire to live without fear, he is not slain by a desire worthy of blame. Thus we have not yet discovered why this deed is evil. For we agreed that all evil deeds are evil for no other reason except that they are done through lust, that is, through blameworthy desire.

29   *E.*   At this point the man who killed his master seems to be condemned unjustly. Yet I would not dare to say this, had I any other answer.

A.   Is it not like this, that you persuaded yourself such a great crime should be unpunished before you considered whether the slave desired to be free of the fear of his master

30   only to satisfy his own lusts? For to wish to live without fear is not only the desire of good men, but the desire of all evil men as well. However the difference is this: that the good seek it by turning their love away from those things which cannot be possessed without the risk of losing them. Evil men, however, try to remove obstacles so that they may safely rest in their enjoyment of these things, and so live a life full of evil and crime, which would be better named death.

31   *E.*   I have come to my senses. Now I am glad that I clearly know the nature of that blameworthy desire called lust [*libido*]. It now appears to be the love of those things which a man can lose against his will.

V.
What of the legal killing of criminals?

E.   Therefore, let us now investigate, if you will, whether lust is also the dominant factor in sacrilege—most cases of which, we note, are committed because of superstition.

32   *A.*   Isn't that problem premature? For first we ought to discuss, I think, whether there is any lust in the case where

an attacking enemy or an assassin in ambush is killed for the sake of life, liberty, or chastity.

E. How can I think that men lack lust who fight for the things that they can lose against their will? Or, if they cannot lose these things, what need is there to go as far as murdering a man for them?

A. Therefore, the law is not just which grants a traveler 33 the power to kill a highway robber so that he himself may not be killed; or which grants a man or woman the right to slay, if they can, an assailant before he can do violence. Indeed, the law even commands a soldier to kill the enemy, and if the soldier refrains from the slaughter, he is punished by his commander. We shall not, shall we, dare say that these laws are unjust—or rather, are not laws at all, for I think that a law that is not just is not a law.

E. Surely, I think that a law is quite safe from this 34 accusation if it permits the people it rules to do lesser evils so as to avoid greater ones. It is much better that the man who plots against another's life be killed than the man who is defending his life. It is also much worse for an innocent person to be violated than for the assailant to be killed by the person whom he tried to attack. Indeed, in killing the enemy, the soldier is the agent of the law. Thus he merely fulfills his duty without any trace of lust. Furthermore, the 35 law which has been passed to protect the people cannot itself be accused of lust. Surely the man who passed it—if he did so at God's command, that is, if the law is what eternal justice commands—can do so without any lust whatsoever. And even if he did make the law out of some kind of lust, it does not follow from this that one's obedience to the law is tainted with lust, since a good law can be made by an evil man.

If a man seizes tyrannical power, for example, and accepts 36 a bribe from some interested person to pass a law that no one may take a woman by force, even for marriage, this law will not be evil, though the man who made it was unjust and corrupt. Therefore, it is possible to obey without lust the law ordering that an enemy's violence be repulsed with equal violence for the protection of the citizens. The same thing can be said in regard to all the officials who, for the sake of

37   law and order, are subject to any authority. But even though the law is blameless, I do not understand how these men can be, when the law does not force them to kill, but leaves it in their power. They are free not to kill anyone for those things which they can lose against their will, and which they ought not therefore to love.

Concerning life, perhaps there is some question whether or not it can be taken in any way from the soul when the body is slain. But if life can be taken away, then it is to be despised. If life cannot be taken away, then there is nothing to fear.

38   As to chastity, who indeed would doubt that it is fixed in the spirit itself, since it is a virtue? Hence, not even chastity can be taken away by a violent assailant. Therefore, whatever he who is killed was about to take away is not at all in our power; so that I do not understand how it can be called our own. Thus I do not blame the law which permits such aggressors to be slain; yet I do not know how I would defend the man who kills.

39.   *A.*   Much less can I discover why you should seek to defend men whom no law holds to be guilty.

E.   No public, man-made law, perhaps; still, I do not know whether they are not held guilty by some stronger, very secret law, if all things are governed by divine providence. How then, before divine providence, are these men free of sin when they are stained by human blood for the sake of

40   things they ought to despise? I think, therefore, that the law that is written to rule the people is right to permit these acts, while divine providence punishes them. The law of the people deals with acts it must punish in order to keep peace among ignorant men, insofar as deeds can be governed by man; these other sins have other suitable punishments, from which, I think, only wisdom can free us.

41   *A.*   I praise and approve this distinction that you have made. It is incomplete and imperfect; nevertheless it is full

of faith, and aims at the sublime. The law which is made to govern states seems to you to make many concessions and to leave unpunished things which are avenged nonetheless by divine providence—and rightly so. But because it does not do all things, it does not thereby follow that what it does do is to be condemned.

VI.
Eternal law and human law.

A.   But let us examine carefully, if you will, how far   42
evil deeds are to be punished by the law that governs people in this life. Then let us see what remains, to be punished by divine providence inevitably and in secret.

E.   I should like to, if only it might be possible to reach a conclusion in such a great question. For I think the problem limitless.

A.   Yes, but have courage; lean upon piety and follow   43
the paths of reason. There is nothing so hard and difficult that it cannot be made clear and obvious by God's help. Let us take up our investigation, then, depending on Him and praying for his help. First tell me whether the law that is published in writing is helpful to men living in this life.

E.   Of course it is, for nations and states are composed   44
of these men.

A.   Are these men and nations of such a nature that they are completely eternal, neither passing away nor changing, or are they mutable and subject to time?

E.   This race is mutable, surely, and a prey to time. Who would doubt it?

A.   Therefore, if a nation is well ordered and serious,   45
a most watchful guardian of the common interest [*communis utilitas*] whose every citizen places the public good above his private interests, is not the law rightly made under which the people are allowed to elect magistrates of their own choice through whom their own welfare—that is, the public welfare—is administered?

    E.   Yes, it is.

46   *A.*   Furthermore, if this same nation gradually becomes depraved, preferring private welfare to public welfare, buying and selling votes, being corrupted by men who love power, and finally turning its government over to evil men and criminals, isn't it right that at such a time a good man, who is outstanding and has the greatest ability, should take the power of conferring offices from this people and reduce the government to a few noblemen or even to one?

    E.   It is right.

47   *A.*   Therefore, although these two laws seem to be opposed to each other in that the one gives to the people the power of conferring offices and the other takes it away, and although the second law is made so that both laws cannot exist at the same time in the same state, still we would not say, would we, that either law is unjust and ought not to be in force?

    E.   By no means.

48   *A.*   Therefore, if you agree, let us call a law temporal when, although it is just, it can justly be changed in the course of time.

    E.   Let us agree to this term.

    A.   What of the law called the highest reason [*summa ratio*], which ought always to be obeyed, the law through which evil men deserve a wretched life and good men a happy one, and through which, finally, the law that we have just called temporal is rightly passed and rightly changed? Can anyone who understands it think it is not immutable and 49 eternal? Can it ever be unjust that the evil are wretched and the good happy, or that the well-ordered and serious nation should elect its own officials while the wicked nation should be deprived of this power?

    E.   I see that this law is eternal and immutable.

50   *A.*   I think too that you understand that in temporal law there is nothing just and lawful which men have not derived from eternal law. If a nation at one time confers offices justly and at another time, still quite justly, does not confer offices,

this change, although it is temporal, is just; for it has been derived from eternal law, under which it is always just for a serious people to confer offices and for a fickle people to be unable to do so. Or do you hold another point of view?

E.   I agree.

A.   To put in a few words, as best I can, the notion of   51 eternal law that has been impressed upon our minds: it is that law by which it is just that everything be ordered in the highest degree [*ordinatissima*]. If you have an objection, state it now.

E.   I have no objection, for you speak the truth.

A.   Therefore, although there is one law according to which all the temporal laws for governing men are changed, the eternal law itself cannot be changed, can it?

E.   I understand that it cannot be changed. No force, no chance, no misfortune can ever bring it about that it is not just for everything to be ordered in the highest degree.

VII.
Eternal law and the highest ordering of human life. Living and knowing that one is alive.

A.   Now let us see how man himself may be most or-   52 dered within. For a nation consists of men, united under one law which, as I have said, is temporal. Tell me: are you very sure that you are alive?

E.   What could be more certain than this?

A.   Can you make the distinction that it is one thing to live and another to know that one lives?

E.   I know that no one, unless he is living, knows that he is alive. Yet I do not know whether or not everything that lives knows it is alive.

A.   How I wish that it were as easy to know that beasts   53 lack reason as to believe so! Then our discussion might pass quickly on from this point. But since you say that you do not know, you start me on a long discourse. This point is not such that we can pass over it and go on toward our goal with-

out sacrificing the rational conclusiveness which I think our
54 argument requires. Tell me, then, since you have often seen
beasts tamed by men—that is, not only the body of the beast,
but even its soul,[1] has been made subject to man, so that it
serves man's will by a kind of sense and habit—tell me
whether you think it possible that a beast, however fierce or
huge or cunning, might try in its turn to make a man subject
to itself, even though it can destroy a man's body by force or
stealth?

E.   I agree that this is by no means possible.

55   A.   Good. But then tell me, since it is evident that man
is easily outdone by most beasts in strength and other physical attributes, what is it in which a man so excels that no
beast can rule him, whereas man can rule many beasts? Is it
perhaps what is usually called reason [*ratio*] or understanding
[*intellegentia*]?

56   E.   I can discover nothing else, since that by which we
excel beasts is in the spirit. If they were inanimate, I would
say that we were superior because we have a spirit. But since
they are animate [*animalia*], what term can I use more appropriate than "reason" to designate what it is which their spirits
lack so that they are subordinate to us, and which is present
in ours so that we are superior to them? For this is by no
means an insignificant thing, as everyone knows.

57   A.   See how, with God's help, we have easily accomplished a task which men think is most difficult. For I confess to you that I had thought this point, which I now understand has been settled, would hold us up for as long a time as
all those we have considered from the beginning of our discussion. Now remember this conclusion so that it may form
the connecting link in our subsequent remarks; for I believe
you realize that what we say we know is nothing else than
what we have perceived through reason.

---

1 The consistent translation of *anima* as soul, *animus* as spirit, and
mens as mind, though arbitrary and not entirely satisfactory (especially
where Augustine does not keep the three distinct) will indicate Augustine's exact wording.

E.   Yes.   58

A.   Therefore, whoever knows that he is alive does not lack reason.

E.   That follows.

A.   Yet beasts are alive and, as we have just now seen, they are without reason.

E.   Obviously.

A.   So you now know what you said you did not know: not everything that lives knows that it lives, although everything that knows that it lives is necessarily alive.

E.   I am in doubt no longer. Go on to the next point: 59
I have now learned that it is one thing to be alive and quite another to know that one is alive.

A.   Which of these two things do you think is more excellent?

E.   Why, clearly, the knowledge of life [*scientia vitae*].

A.   Do you think that the knowledge of life is better than life itself? Or perhaps you understand that a certain higher and truer life consists in the knowledge of life, which no one can have except those who have understanding? For what is understanding except living more clearly and perfectly by the very light of the mind? Therefore, unless I am deceived, you have not set something else above life, but rather have set a better life above mere life.

E.   You have understood and explained my view very   60
well—provided knowledge can never be evil.

A.   I judge that knowledge can in no way be evil unless we change the meaning of the word and confuse knowledge [*scientia*] with experience [*experientia*]. Experience is not always good, as when we experience punishment. Yet how can what is properly and strictly called knowledge be evil, since it is acquired by reason and understanding?

E.   I, too, make this distinction. Proceed with the argument.

VIII.
Reason should be master in human life.

61   *A.*   This is what I mean: whatever it is that sets man above beast—whether it is called mind or spirit [*spiritus*] (or, more correctly, both, since we find both in the Holy Scriptures)—if it controls and commands whatever else man consists of, then man is ordered in the highest degree. We see that we have many things in common not only with beasts, but even with trees and plants. Trees, though they are on the lowest plane of life, take nourishment, grow, reproduce, and become strong. Furthermore, beasts see, hear, and can perceive corporeal things by touch, taste, and smell more keenly

62   than we. Add to this energy, power, strength of limb, speed, and agility of bodily motion. In all of these faculties we excel some, equal others, and to some are inferior.

Things of this sort we clearly share with beasts. Indeed, to seek the pleasures of the body and to avoid harm constitute

63   the entire activity of a beast's life. There are other things which do not seem to fall to the lot of beasts, but which nevertheless are not the highest attributes of man: jesting and laughing, for example, which anyone who judges human nature correctly judges to be human, though he rates them low. Again, there are the love of praise and glory and the desire for power; while beasts do not have these, nevertheless

64   we are not to be judged better than beasts because of them. For this craving, when not subject to reason, makes men wretched, and no one has ever thought himself superior to another because of his own wretchedness. When reason is master of these emotions [*motus animae*], a man may be said to be well ordered [*ordinatus*]. No order in which the better are subject to the worse can be called right, or can even be called order at all. Do you agree?

65   *E.*   It is obvious.

A.   Therefore, when reason, whether mind or spirit, rules the irrational emotions, then there exists in man the

very mastery which the law that we know to be eternal pre-
scribes.

E.   I understand and follow.

IX.
What distinguishes the wise from the foolish?

A.   When a man is so constituted and ordered, do you   66
not consider him wise?

E.   No one could be considered wise except such a man.

A.   I imagine too that you realize that many men are
fools.

E.   This is quite certain.

A.   If a fool is the opposite of a wise man, and we know   67
what a wise man is, you surely know what a fool is.

E.   Who could not see that a fool is a man in whom the
mind does not have full mastery?

A.   What are we to say of a fool? That he lacks a mind?
Or that the mind, though it exists in him, does not have
mastery?

E.   The latter.

A.   I would like to hear from you on what basis you feel
that there is a mind in a man when it does not exert its
authority.

E.   I wish you would take over the argument, for it is
not easy for me to maintain my position in the face of your
attack.

A.   At least it is easy for you to remember what we have   68
just said, how beasts are tamed by men and obey men; the
reverse could happen, as the argument showed, were it not for
the fact that man is superior in some way. We found that the
superiority was not in the body. Since the superiority plainly
lay in the spirit, we knew nothing else to call it except reason [*ratio*]. Then we recalled that reason can be called mind
or spirit [*spiritus*]. If reason is one thing and mind another,
surely we agree that only mind can use reason, so that we
have proved that he who has reason cannot be without mind.

69   *E.*   I remember this well, and I accept it.

     A.   Do you believe that the masters of beasts cannot be masters unless they are wise? I call those men wise whom the truth commands to be called wise, that is, those who are at peace because they have made lust subject to the rule of the mind.

     E.   It is absurd to think those men wise who are commonly called animal trainers, or even shepherds, plowmen, or charioteers. We see that animals obey these men, and that by their work the wild animals are tamed.

70   *A.*   You have the clearest evidence to show that mind can be present in man, and yet not have control. Indeed it is present in men, for men do things that could not be done without mind; yet the mind does not have control, for they are foolish. Rule by the human mind, it has been acknowledged, belongs only to wise men.

     E.   I am amazed that, though all this was proved by earlier arguments, I could not think what I should answer.

X.
No one can force the soul to be a slave to lust.

     E.   But let us take up some other arguments. We have already proved that governance by the human mind is human wisdom, and that the mind may not always rule.

71   *A.*   Do you think that any lust can overpower that mind to which we know dominion over lusts has been granted by eternal law? I myself do not think so. For the order [of the universe] would not be the most excellent possible if the weaker commanded the stronger. Therefore, it necessarily follows that the mind is more powerful than desire [*cupiditas*], because it is right and just that it should rule desire.

     E.   I think so too.

72   *A.*   We would not hesitate, would we, to prefer every virtue to every vice, so that the stronger and more invincible a virtue is, the better and nobler it is?

     E.   Of course not.

A. Therefore, no vicious spirit overcomes the spirit armed by virtue.

E. Very true.

A. I think that you will not deny that any spirit whatever is better and more powerful than any body.

E. No one denies it who sees, as he easily may, that a living substance is to be preferred to a non-living one, and that the thing that gives life is to be preferred to that which receives it.

A. So much the less, then, does the body, whatever it 73 may be, overcome the spirit endowed with virtue.

E. Obviously.

A. What then? Can the just spirit, and the mind that is watchful over its own right and rule, throw down from its citadel another mind which rules with justice and virtue, and subjugate it to lust?

E. By no means; not only because the same excellence is in each, but also because the former mind will fall away from justice and become sinful; it will become weaker in trying to make the other sinful.

A. You understand well. It remains for you to answer 74 this, if you can: do you think there is anything more excellent than a rational and wise mind?

E. Nothing, I think, except God.

A. This is my opinion too. But though we accept this with the strongest faith, understanding it is a very difficult matter. This is not the time to take it up, since our investigation of this question must be careful and systematic.

XI.
A soul merits punishment when it voluntarily submits to lust.

A. For the present, we can be certain that whatever be 75 that nature which, by right, is superior to the mind strong in virtue, it cannot be unjust. Therefore, even though it may have the power to do so, it will not force the mind to serve lust.

E.   No one would hesitate to admit this.

76   *A.*   Since, because of justice, whatever is equal or superior to the mind that possesses virtue and is in control does not make the mind a slave to lust; and since, because of its weakness, whatever is inferior to the mind cannot do this (as the things we have established prove)—therefore it follows that nothing can make the mind a companion of desire except its own will and free choice [*voluntas et liberum arbitrium*].

E.   I can see no other conclusion.

77   *A.*   It follows, then, that you think it just to suffer punishment for so great a sin.

E.   I cannot deny it.

A.   What about this, then? Is this in itself to be considered a trifling punishment? Lust dominates the mind, despoils it of the wealth of its virtue, and drags it, poor and needy, now this way and now that; now approving and even defending what is false as though it were true, now disapproving what it previously defended, and rushing on to other falsities; now refusing assent and fearing clear reasoning; now despairing of fully discovering the truth and clinging to the deep obscurities of stupidity; now struggling into the light of understanding and falling back again from weariness.

78   Meanwhile the reign of lust rages tyrannically and distracts the life and whole spirit of man with many conflicting storms of terror, desire, anxiety, empty and false happiness, torture because of the loss of something that he used to love, eagerness to possess what he does not have, grievances for injuries received, and fires of vengeance. Wherever he turns, greed amasses, extravagance wastes, ambition entices, pride bloats, envy twists, sloth buries, obstinacy goads, submissiveness harasses, and all the other innumerable things that throng and busy themselves in the kingdom of lust. Can we think that this is not punishment which, as you see, all must endure who do not cling to wisdom?

79   *E.*   Indeed I do think that this is a severe penalty and a completely just one, if someone already at the height of

wisdom chooses to descend and serve lust. But it is uncertain whether there can be anyone who has willed or who wills
to do this. For although we believe that man was perfectly
formed by God and placed by Him in a life of blessedness,
and that man himself fell, by his own will alone, subject to
the hardships of mortal life—although I hold to this with the
firmest faith, I have not yet grasped it with my understanding.
If now you think that a careful consideration of this question
should be postponed, you do so against my will.

XII.
The lustful justly suffer in the present life.

E.   But what perplexes me most of all is this: Why   80
should we suffer bitter punishment of this kind when, though
assuredly we are foolish, we have never been wise? How can
we be said to endure these things deservedly for having deserted the citadel of virtue and chosen to be slaves of lust? If
you are able to make this clear by discussion, I would on no
account be willing for you to postpone the question.

A.   You say this as though you had clearly proved that   81
we never were wise. You are thinking only of the time since
we were born into this life. But because wisdom lies in the
spirit, there is a great mystery which we must study in its
appropriate place: whether the spirit, before its union with
the body, lived in another life, and whether at such a time
it lived in a condition of wisdom. Nevertheless, this does not
prevent us from explaining as far as possible the problem at
hand. For I ask you: do you have a will?   82

E.   I don't know.

A.   Do you want to know?

E.   I don't know that either.

A.   Then ask me nothing more.

E.   Why?

A.   Because I ought not to answer your questions, unless
you have a will to know what you ask. And also, unless it is
your will to arrive at wisdom, there is no point to discussing

things of this kind with you. Finally, you cannot be my friend if you do not will things to go well for me. And surely, with regard to yourself: do you think you have no will to be happy?

83   *E.*   I yield; it cannot be denied that we have a will. Now let us see how you proceed from this point.

A.   All right, but first tell me whether you think that you have a good will.

E.   What is a good will?

A.   A will by which we seek to live rightly and honorably and to come to the highest wisdom. Only see whether you do not desire an upright and honorable life, or whether you do not earnestly want to be wise. And would you dare to deny with certainty that we have a good will when we wish for these things?

84   *E.*   I deny none of these points, and I admit besides that I have, not only a will, but even a good will.

A.   What value, I ask, do you set on this will? You would not, would you, compare it to riches or honors or pleasures of the body, or even all of these together?

E.   God forbid such wicked madness!

85   *A.*   Should we not, therefore, rejoice that we have something in our spirit which I call good will, compared to which the things we have just mentioned are worthless, though we see many men shrink from no trouble or peril to acquire them?

E.   Yes, we ought to rejoice very much.

A.   Do you think that men who do not feel this joy suffer only a slight loss when they lose so great a good?

E.   They suffer, rather, the greatest loss.

86   *A.*   Now I think you see that it lies in the power of our own will to enjoy or else to lack such a great and true good. For what lies more truly in the power of the will than the will itself? Whoever has a good will certainly has a thing to be preferred by far to all earthly realms and all pleasures of the body. Whoever does not have a good will surely lacks that very thing which is more excellent than all the goods not

in our power, that thing which the will alone, in itself, may give. So while a man thinks that he is very unhappy if he has lost his fine reputation, great wealth, or various goods of the body, would you not consider him extremely unhappy even if he had an abundance of such things? For he is clinging to things that he can very easily lose and that he does not have while he wants them; he lacks, moreover, the good will which is not to be compared to these and which, though it is so great a good, he needs only to will in order to possess. 87

E.   Quite right.

A.   Rightly and deservedly are foolish men afflicted by unhappiness of this sort, even if they never were wise (for this point is uncertain and obscure). 88

E.   I agree.

XIII.
It is by willing that we live a happy or an unhappy life.

A.   Next let us consider whether you think that prudence is the knowledge of what should be desired and what should be avoided. 89

E.   I do think so.

A.   Is not fortitude that condition of the soul by which we despise all hardships and losses of things that have not been placed under our control?

E.   I think it is.

A.   Furthermore, temperance is a quality which checks and controls the desire for those things that it is base to desire. Or do you disagree?

E.   No, I think as you do.

A.   Is not justice the virtue according to which each man receives what is his due? 90

E.   I have no other notion of justice.

A.   Then whoever has a good will, the excellence of which we have been discussing for a long time, will embrace this one virtue with a devotion that considers that there is nothing better. Let him take delight in it; let him enjoy it and be happy. When we consider justice and estimate how great it is and how it cannot be taken or stolen from a man against his will, we cannot doubt, can we, that such a man is a foe to all the things that oppose this one good?

E.   He is, of necessity, completely opposed to them.

91   A.   Should we think a man endowed with no prudence at all, if he realizes that prudence is to be desired while those things which oppose it are to be avoided?

E.   I think that such a man is by no means without prudence.

A.   Right. But why do we attribute fortitude to him as well? Surely he cannot love and judge to be of great value all these things which are not in our power. For they are loved by an evil will, which he must oppose as an enemy of his dearest possession. Since, moreover, he does not dare to love these things, he does not grieve when they are lost; rather, he despises them utterly. For this he needs fortitude—as I said, with your agreement.

92   E.   I grant this. I do not know anyone whom I could call more truly brave than the man who foregoes, with a calm and tranquil mind, the things that we are not allowed to acquire or keep; and we have shown without doubt that the brave man does just this.

A.   Next, see whether we can deprive him of temperance, since this is the virtue which restrains lust. What is as hostile to the good will as lust? From this you know that this man who loves his own good will resists and opposes lust in every way he can, and therefore can justly be called temperate.

E.   Go on. I agree.

93   A.   There remains justice; and I certainly do not see how this man can lack justice. For whoever possesses and loves a good will and, as I have said, opposes the things that are hostile to it, is incapable of wishing evil for anyone. So it will follow that he does not harm anyone—and this can be the case only if he gives to each man his due. Moreover, when I said that this was the nature of justice, I think you remember that you agreed.

E.   I do remember; and I admit that we find, in the man who reckons and esteems the good will to be of great value, all four of the virtues that you described to me (and to which I agreed) a little while ago.

A.   What then prevents us from granting that his life 94 is praiseworthy?

E.   Nothing. Everything urges us, and even forces us, to grant this.

A.   What about the unhappy life? Is there any way in which you can escape the conclusion that it is to be avoided?

E.   I do not think there is anything else to do.

A.   But surely you do not think that a praiseworthy life should be avoided?

E.   Indeed, I think that it should eagerly be sought.

A.   Therefore, the life that is praiseworthy is not unhappy.

E.   That follows.

A.   So far as I can see, it is not difficult for you to agree that the life that is not unhappy is the happy life?

E.   Obviously.

A.   We agree that the happy man is the lover of his own 95 good will, a man who spurns, by comparison, every other good, which can still be lost even when the will to keep it remains.

E.   Why should we not agree to this, since it follows necessarily from the points we established earlier?

A.   You understand well. But tell me, please: to love one's good will and to esteem it as highly as we have said— is this not the good will itself?

E.   Yes.

A.   But if we are correct to consider this man happy, are we not correct to consider the man who is of contrary will unhappy?

E.   Correct.

A.   What, therefore, is the cause of our doubting (even 96 if we never have been wise before) that it is by will that we deserve and live a praiseworthy and happy life, and by will that we deserve and live a disgraceful and unhappy life?

E.   I admit that we have come to this conclusion by means of sure and undeniable arguments.

97   *A.*   Let us look at something else: I believe that you remember how we defined good will. I think we said that it is that by which we seek to live rightly and honorably.

E.   Yes, I remember this.

A.   Therefore, if we should love and embrace with our will the good will, and place it before all other things that we cannot keep even if we will to do so, then those virtues, as reason demonstrates, will dwell in our spirit, and to possess them is to live rightly and honorably. From this it is established that whoever wants to live rightly and honorably, if his will for this surpasses his will for temporal goods, achieves this great good so easily that to have what he wills is nothing other than the act of willing.

98   *E.*   Truly, I can scarcely keep from shouting for joy when I see that such a great good has arisen before me, and has so easily been established.

A.   When this very joy, born out of the attainment of this good, calmly, peacefully, and continually lifts up the spirit, it is called the happy life—unless you think that to live happily is something other than to rejoice in true and sure goods.

E.   No; I agree with you.

XIV.
Why are so few men happy when all want to be?

99   *A.*   Good. But do you think that every man does not in every way want and desire the happy life?

E.   Who doubts that every man wants a happy life?

A.   Why then do not all men achieve it? For we have said and agreed between us that it is by the will that men merit a happy life, and by the will that they merit an unhappy one. Thus they merit what they receive. But now arises some sort of conflict, and unless we watch carefully, it will upset our previous reasoning, which was so careful and cer-

tain. For how, by will, does anyone suffer an unhappy life   100
when no one by any means wants to live unhappily? Or how
does a man gain a happy life through his will, when although
all want to be happy, there are so many unhappy men? Is this
the result of the fact that it is one thing to wish rightly or
wrongly, and another thing to merit something through a
good or evil will? Those who are happy, who also ought to be
good, are not happy because they desire to live happily, which
even evil men desire, but rather because they will to live
rightly—which evil men do not. Thus it is no wonder that un- 101
happy men do not attain what they want, that is, a happy
life, for they do not also will to live rightly—a thing which
accompanies the happy life, and without which the happy life
can be neither merited nor attained by anyone. The eternal
law, to which it is time now to turn our attention, established
with immutable firmness the point that merit lies in the will,
while happiness and unhappiness are a matter of reward and
punishment.

Thus when we say that men are unhappy because of their   102
will, we do not mean that they wish to be unhappy, but that
they are in that state of will where unhappiness must result
even if they do not want it. So it is not inconsistent with our
previous reasoning to say that all men wish to be happy, but
all men cannot be, since not all possess that will to live
rightly to which the happy life is due. Do you have any objections to raise?

E.   I have none.

XV.
The love of temporal things and the love of
eternal things. Unhappiness stems from
lust after temporal things.

E.   But let us see how these points are related to our   103
question about the two laws.

A.   Yes. First tell me whether the man who loves to live
rightly and is so delighted by the righteous life that he finds

it not only right, but even sweet and pleasing—tell me whether
that man loves and holds most precious the law according to
which a happy life is allotted to the good will, and an unhappy one to the evil will?

E.   He loves it completely and utterly, for it is by following that very law that he lives thus.

104   A.   When he loves this law, does he love something
changeable and temporal, or unchanging and eternal?

E.   Eternal, surely, and immutable.

A.   Can those who persist in an evil will, but who still
desire to be happy, love the very law by which unhappiness is
justly meted out to them?

E.   No, not by any means.

A.   Do they love nothing else?

E.   On the contrary, they love many things—the very
things, in fact, that the evil will persists in obtaining and in
clinging to.

105   A.   I think that you mean riches, honors, pleasures, bodily beauty, and all the other things which their will alone
cannot obtain for them, and which they can lose, although
they are unwilling to.

E.   These are the things.

A.   You do not think, do you, that these things are
eternal, since you see that they are liable to the vicissitudes of
time?

E.   Who but a madman would think so!

106   A.   Since it is clear that some men love eternal things
while others love temporal ones, and since we have agreed
that there exist two laws, the eternal and the temporal—if
you know anything about equity, who do you judge ought to
be subject to eternal law, and who to temporal?

E.   I think that what you ask is obvious. It is apparent
that happy men, because they love eternal things, act under
the eternal law, while unhappy men are subject to the temporal law.

107   A.   Your judgment is correct, provided that you firmly
believe what reason has now clearly demonstrated: that those

who serve temporal law cannot be free of the eternal law from which, we said, are derived all the things that are just or justly changed; and those who abide by the eternal law through good will do not need temporal law. You understand this quite well, it appears.

E.   I do.

A.   The eternal law, therefore, orders us to turn our love away from temporal things, and to turn it in its purity to the eternal. 108

E.   Yes, it does.

A.   What then do you think that the temporal law commands, except that men should possess these things which may be called ours for a time (when men cling to them out of desire) by that right by which peace and human society are preserved—insofar as they can be preserved amid these circumstances? And these are, first, the body, together with what are called its goods, such as good health, keen senses, strength, beauty; certain of these are needed in the useful arts and therefore are to be more highly valued, while others are of less value. Next there is freedom—not, indeed, true freedom, which is reserved for those who are happy and who abide by eternal law; rather, I am speaking now of that freedom which men who have no masters think they possess, and which men who wish to be free of human masters desire. Next, there are parents, brothers, husband or wife, children, kindred, relatives, friends, and those who are bound to us by some bond of intimacy. Then, too, there is the state itself, which is usually held to have the place of a parent. There are also honors, praise, and what is called popular favor. Lastly, there are possessions [*pecunia*]—a term which includes all the things that we rightfully own, over which we seem to have the power of selling or giving away. 109 110

To explain how the law distributes to each man his own property is difficult and lengthy, and is clearly not at all necessary for what we propose. It is enough to understand that the power exercised by this law extends only to the taking away and removal of these things, or some of them, from 111 those whom it punishes. It maintains order through fear, twisting and turning to what it wants the minds of those unhappy men whom it has been adapted to rule. Since men fear to lose temporal goods, in using them they observe a certain moderation suited to the bond of whatever kind of society can be

112   established by men of this sort. They do not punish the sin of loving temporal goods except when the temporal goods are dishonestly taken from others. Therefore, see how we have come to the point you thought so far away; for we had planned to inquire how far the law which governs states and the people of this world has the right to punish.

E.   I see that we have come to this point.

A.   Therefore, you also understand that if men did not love what can be taken away from them against their will, there would be no punishment, either through wrong done to them or through retribution exacted from them for some wrong.

E.   I understand this also.

113   A.   Thus some men make evil use of these things, and others make good use. And the man who makes evil use clings to them with love and is entangled by them (that is, he becomes subject to those things which ought to be subject to him, and creates for himself goods whose right and proper use require that he himself be good); but the man who uses these rightly proves that they are indeed goods, though not for him (for they do not make him good or better, but become better because of him). Therefore he is not attached to them by love, lest he make them limbs, as it were, of his spirit (which happens if he loves them), and lest they weaken him with pain and wasting when they begin to be cut off from him. Instead, let him be above temporal things completely. He must be ready to possess and control them, and even more ready to lose and not to possess them. Since this is so, you do not think, do you, that silver or gold should be blamed because of greedy men, or food and wine because of gluttons and drunkards, or womanly beauty because of adulterers and fornicators? And so on with other things, especially since you

may see a doctor use fire well, and the poisoner using bread for his crime.

E. This is most true. The things themselves are not to be blamed, but rather the men who make evil use of them.

XVI.
Summary and conclusion.

A. Good. Since now we have begun, I think, to under- 114
stand how strong eternal law is and how far temporal law may go in exacting punishment, we have discovered that there are two kinds of things, eternal and temporal. Two kinds of men, as well, have been clearly and sufficiently distinguished: those who pursue and love eternal things, and those who pursue and love temporal things. We have established, more-over, that what each man chooses to pursue and to love lies in his own will, and that the mind cannot be deposed from the citadel of mastery or from right order by anything except the will. And it is clear that things themselves are not to be blamed when someone makes evil use of them; rather, the man who makes evil use of them is to be blamed.

Let us return, if you will, to the question proposed at the beginning of our conversation and see if it has been answered. For we began by asking what it is to do evil, and our whole 115
discussion has arisen out of this question. Therefore, we must now turn to consider the question whether to do evil is not to neglect eternal things—those things which the mind enjoys and perceives of itself, and which it cannot lose as long as it loves them—and to follow, as if they were great and won-drous, temporal things, which are perceived by the body, the basest part of man, and which can never be certain. All evil deeds—that is, sins—are, I think, included in this one class. I am waiting to hear what you think.

E. It is as you say; I agree. All sins are included under 116
this one class: when someone is turned away from divine things that are truly everlasting, toward things that change and are uncertain. These things have been rightly placed in

their own order and complete the universe through their own peculiar beauty; but nevertheless, it is characteristic of the perverse and disordered spirit to be a slave to the pursuit of the things which divine order and law have prescribed should follow its own bidding.

117   At the same time, I think we have solved and answered the problem that arose after the question of what evil is: namely, why we commit evil. Unless I am mistaken, reason has shown that we commit evil through free choice of the will. But I question whether free will—through which, it has been shown, we have the power to sin—ought to have been given to us by Him who made us. For it seems that we would not have been able to sin, if we did not have free will. And it is to be feared that in this way God may appear to be the cause of our evil deeds.

118   *A.*   Do not be anxious over this. We must find some other opportunity to search this question out carefully, for the time has come to bring our present discussion to a close. I want you to believe that we have, as it were, knocked at the doors of great mysteries into which we must inquire. When we begin to enter their sanctuaries, with God leading us, you will surely recognize what a difference there is between this discussion and those which are to follow, and how much the latter will surpass the former, not only in the keenness of thought they demand, but also in the majesty of their subject matter and the clear light of their truth. May there be enough piety in us for divine Providence to allow us to follow the end the course we have set out upon!

    E.   I yield to your will and most willingly join you in your proposal.

BOOK TWO

I.
Why did God give freedom of the will to men, since it is by this that men sin?

Evodius.   Now, if possible, explain to me why God gave   1
man free choice of the will, since if he had not received it
he would not be able to sin.

Augustine.   Are you perfectly sure that God gave to man
what you think ought not to have been given?

E.   As far as I seem to understand the discussion in the
first book, we have freedom of will, and could not sin if we
were without it.

A.   I, too, remember that this was made clear to us. But
I just asked you whether you know that it was God who gave
us that which we possess, through which it is clear that we
commit sin.

E.   No one else. For we are from Him, and whether we   2
sin or whether we do right, we earn reward or punishment
from Him.

A.   I want to ask, as well: do you know this clearly, or
do you believe it willingly without really knowing it, because
you are prompted by authority?

E.   I admit that at first I trusted authority on this
point. But what can be more true than that all good proceeds
from God, that everything just is good, and that it is just to
punish sinners and to reward those who do right? From this it
follows that through God sinners are afflicted with unhappiness, and those who do right endowed with happiness.

A.   I do not object, but let me ask another question: 3
how do you know that we are from God? You did not answer
that; instead, you explained that we merit punishment and
reward from God.

35

E.   The answer to *that* question, too, is clear, if for no other reason than the fact that, as we have already agreed, God punishes sins. All justice is from God, and it is not the role of justice to punish foreigners, although it is the role

4   of goodness to bestow benefits on them. Thus it is clear that we belong to God, since He is not only most generous in bestowing benefits upon us, but also most just in punishing us. Also, we can understand that man is from God through the fact, which I proposed and you conceded, that every good is from God. For man himself, insofar as he is a man, is a good, because he can live rightly when he so wills.

5   *A.*   If this is so, the question that you proposed is clearly answered. If man is a good, and cannot act rightly unless he wills to do so, then he must have free will, without which he cannot act rightly. We must not believe that God gave us free will so that we might sin, just because sin is committed through free will. It is sufficient for our question, why free will should have been given to man, to know that without it man cannot live rightly. That it was given for this reason can be understood from the following: if anyone uses free

6   will for sinning, he incurs divine punishment. This would be unjust if free will had been given not only that man might live rightly, but also that he might sin. For how could a man justly incur punishment who used free will to do the thing for which it was given? When God punishes a sinner, does He not seem to say, "Why have you not used free will for the

7   purpose for which I gave it to you, to act rightly"? Then too, if man did not have free choice of will, how could there exist the good according to which it is just to condemn evildoers and reward those who act rightly? What was not done by will would be neither evildoing nor right action. Both punishment and reward would be unjust if man did not have free will. Moreover, there must needs be justice both in punishment and in reward, since justice is one of the goods that are from God. Therefore, God must needs have given free will to man.

II.
If freedom is a good, given for good use, why can it be turned to evil uses?

E.   I concede now that God gave free will. But I beg   8
you, don't you think that, if free will was given so that man
might act rightly, it should not be possible to use it to sin?
For example, justice itself was given so that man might live
well. No one can live in evil through his own justice, can he?
In the same way, no one could sin through his will, if the
will is given for acting rightly.

A.   I hope that God will give me the power to answer   9
you, or rather that He will give you power to find the answer
yourself through that very thing which is the highest teacher
of all—the truth within which teaches us. Please tell me
briefly: if you acknowledge as certain what I questioned you
about, namely that God gave us free will, tell me whether we
ought to say that God should not have given what we concede
He did give. If it is uncertain whether He gave free will, we   10
may properly ask whether it was a good gift, so that if we
should discover that it is a good gift, we would discover also
that it was given by Him who gave the soul all good gifts. If,
on the other hand, we should discover that free will is not a
good gift, we would know that He whom it is wicked to
blame did not give it. Yet if it is certain that God Himself
gave free will, however it was given, we must acknowledge
that it neither ought not to have been given, nor has been
given in any other way than it was given; for God gave free
will and His deed can in no wise be justly condemned.

E.   Although I believe this with unshaken faith, never-   11
theless I do not understand it. Therefore, let us take up our
investigation as though everything were uncertain. From the
fact that it is uncertain whether free will was given so that
man might live rightly, since we can sin through free will, it
follows that it becomes uncertain whether free will ought to

have been given. If we do not know that it was given so that
man might live rightly, we also do not know that it ought to
12   have been given. In consequence of this, it is uncertain
whether God gave free will. For if it is uncertain that free
will ought to have been given, it is also uncertain that free
will was given by God, since it is wicked to believe that God
gave anything that should not have been given.

   A.   At least you are certain that God exists.

   E.   I accept even this by faith, and not by reason.

13   *A.*   If any fool who has said in his heart, "There is no
God," [1] should say this to you and be unwilling to believe
with you what you believe, but should want to know whether
your belief was true—would you walk away from the man,
or would you think that he should be persuaded of what you
firmly believe, especially if he was eager to know, and not
just to argue stubbornly?

14   *E.*   Your last question gives me a good hint as to how I
should answer him. Surely, however unreasonable he might
be, he would concede that I ought not to dispute with a sly
and stubborn man about anything at all, let alone such an
important thing. After he granted this, we should first hold
a discussion so that I might believe that he raised the question in the right spirit, and that nothing which would affect
the argument, like trickery or stubborness, lay hidden in him.

15   Then I would prove to him what I think is very easily
proven: how much fairer it is, when he wants another who
does not know to believe him concerning the secrets of his
own spirit which he himself knows—how much fairer it is to
believe that God exists by the authority of the books of those
great men who left written testimony that they lived with
the Son of God, since they wrote that they saw things which
could not have happened if God did not exist. He would be
foolish indeed if he, who wanted me to believe him, were to
blame me for believing them. A man could find no reason
why he should not be willing to imitate what he cannot
justly blame.

[1] Ps. 52:1.

A.   If you think that it is sufficient to judge that we have   16
not been rash in believing such great men on the question
of God's existence, why then, I beg you, don't you think that
we can likewise believe these same men's authority in the
other matters into whose investigation we entered assuming
them to be uncertain and obscure? Then we would have to
toil no further in investigating them.

E.   But we want to know and understand what we believe.

A.   You remember rightly; we cannot abandon the posi-   17
tion we adopted at the beginning of the first discourse. Unless believing is different from understanding, and unless we
first believe the great and divine thing that we desire to
understand, the prophet has said in vain, "Unless you believe,
you shall not understand." [2] Our Lord Himself, by His words   18
and deeds, first urged those whom He called to salvation to
believe. Afterwards, when He spoke about the gift He was to
give to those who believed, He did not say, "This is life eternal so that they may believe." Instead He said, "This is life
eternal that they may know Thee, the one true God and Him
whom Thou didst send, Jesus Christ." [3] Then, to those who
believed, He said, "Seek and you shall find." [4] For what is
believed without being known cannot be said to have been
found, and no one can become fit for finding God unless he
believes first what he shall know afterwards. Therefore, in   19
obedience to the teachings of our Lord, let us seek earnestly.
That which we seek at God's bidding we shall find when He
Himself shows us—as far as it can be found in this life and
by such men as we are. We must believe that these things are
seen and grasped more clearly and fully by better men even
while they dwell in this world, and surely by all good and
devout men after this life. So we must hope and, disdaining
worldly and human things, must love and desire divine
things.

[2] Is. 7:9, Septuagint.
[3] John 17:3.
[4] Matt. 7:7.

III.
To show that God exists, it is necessary to investigate man's consciousness of himself. The bodily senses and the inner sense.

20   *A.*   Let us take up our search in the following order, if you will. First, how is it proved [*manifestum*] that God exists? Second, are all things whatsoever, insofar as they are good, from God? Finally, is free will to be counted as a good? When we have answered these questions, it will be quite clear, I think, whether free will was rightly given. Therefore, to start at the beginning with the most obvious, I will ask you first whether you yourself exist. Are you, perhaps, afraid that you are being deceived by my questioning? But if you did not exist, it would be impossible for you to be deceived.

E.   Let us move on.

21   *A.*   Since it is clear that you exist, and since this would not be clear to you unless you lived, it is also clear that you are alive. So you understand that these two points are absolutely true?

E.   I fully understand.

A.   Then this third point is also clear: you understand.

E.   Yes.

A.   Which of these three things do you think is the best?

E.   Understanding.

A.   Why do you think so?

22   *E.*   Because, while there are these things—to be, to live, and to understand—the stone *is,* and the beast *lives,* yet I think that the stone does not live, nor the beast understand. Furthermore, it is very certain that he who understands both *is* and *lives.* For this reason, I do not hesitate to judge that in which all these three are present to be more perfect than that

23   in which any one is lacking. For what lives, also *is;* but it does not follow that it also understands. Such, I think, is the life of

a beast. Furthermore, what *is* does not necessarily live or understand. I can admit that a dead body *is*, yet no one would say that it lives. Likewise, what does not live surely does not understand.

A. We maintain, then, that the dead body lacks two 24 of these three; the beast, one; and man, none.

E. Yes.

A. We maintain this as well: of these three, what man has in addition to the two others—that is, understanding—is the most excellent. In having this, man consequently also *is* and lives.

E. We also maintain this.

A. Now tell me whether you know that you possess the 25 ordinary bodily senses: sight, hearing, smell, taste, and touch.

E. I know that I possess them.

A. What do you think is the proper object of the sense of sight? That is, what do we perceive by sight?

E. Anything corporeal.

A. We don't perceive hardness and softness by sight, do we?

E. We do not.

A. What then is the proper object of the eyes; what do we perceive with them?

E. Color.

A. The ears?

E. Sound.

A. Smell?

E. Odor.

A. Taste?

E. Flavor.

A. Touch?

E. Soft and hard, smooth and rough, and many other such things.

A. What about the shapes of bodies: large, small, angular, rounded, and others of this kind? Don't we perceive them by touch and sight, so that they can properly be attributed, neither to sight nor to touch alone, but to both?

E.   I understand.

26   *A.*   Therefore, you understand both that each sense has certain obejcts of its own about which it reports, and that some senses have objects in common.

E.   I understand this also.

A.   We cannot, can we, discern by any one sense either what is the proper object of that individual sense, or what all or some senses possess in common among themselves?

E.   Of course not. This is discerned by something within.

A.   Can this be reason, which beasts lack? For it seems to me that by reason we grasp this and know it is so.

27   *E.*   No; I think, rather, that by reason we understand that there is a certain inner sense to which all things are referred by the five familiar senses. For the beast sees by one thing; by another, it avoids or seeks what it has perceived with its sight. For sight lies in its eyes, while the other sense lies within its soul. By this other sense, animals either seek and take (if pleased), or avoid and reject (if annoyed), what 28   they see, hear, and grasp with the other senses. This sense cannot be called either sight, hearing, smell, taste or touch. It is something else which controls all the senses in common. While we grasp this with our reason, we cannot call it reason, since it is clearly to be found in beasts.

29   *A.*   I recognize this, whatever it is, and I do not hesitate to name it "the inner sense." But unless what we perceive by the bodily senses passes beyond the inner sense, we cannot arrive at knowledge [*scientia*]. Whatever we know, we grasp and hold to by reason. Moreover, we know that we cannot perceive colors with our hearing or voices with our eyes, to 30   say nothing of the other senses. When we know this, we know it neither by the eyes, nor by the ears, nor by the inner sense which beasts do not lack. We must not believe that beasts know that light is not perceived by the ears nor a voice by the eyes, for we perceive this only by rational thought and reflection within the soul.

31   *E.*   I cannot say that I am clear about this. What if animals, too, discern that colors cannot be perceived by hear-

ing and voices by sight, by means of that inner sense which you admit they do not lack?

A. You don't think, do you, that animals can discern separately [1] the color which is perceived, or [2] the sense which is in the eyes, or [3] the inner sense in the soul, or [4] reason, by which these things are each distinguished and defined?

E. Of course not.

A. Could reason discern these four things separately 32 and limit them by definition, unless color were referred to reason by the sense belonging to the eyes, and this in turn by the inner sense which controls it, and the inner sense in turn by itself, if nothing else were interposed?

E. I do not see how else it could.

A. Do you see that color is perceived by the sense be- 33 longing to the eyes, and that the sensation itself is not perceived by the same sense? You do not see that you see with one and the same sense by which you see color, do you?

E. Absolutely not.

A. Try also to distinguish these. I believe that you do not deny that [1] color is one thing, that [2] to see color is another, and that [3] when color is not present, it is still another thing to have the sense by which color could be seen if color were present.

E. I do make such a distinction, and admit that they are quite different things.

A. You don't perceive any of these three things, except 34 color, by the eyes, do you?

E. No.

A. Tell me, therefore, how you see the two other things. For you could not distinguish them unless they were seen.

E. I don't know how else. I do know that they exist, but know nothing more.

A. You do not know, therefore, whether it is reason itself, or that life we call the inner sense that excels the bodily senses, or something else?

E. I do not.

35   *A*.   Yet you do know this: that it is not possible to define these things except by reason, and that reason cannot do this except in the case of things which are brought to it to be examined.

E.   That is certain.

A.   Whatever that other thing is by which all that we know can be perceived, it is the servant of reason, to which it brings and reports whatever touches it, so that what is perceived can be distinguished by its own limits and grasped, not only by perception, but also by knowledge.

E.   Yes.

36   *A*.   That very reason which discerns its own servants and the objects that they bring to it, which likewise recognizes the differences between these things and itself, and affirms that it is more powerful than they—that very reason does not comprehend itself by anything other than itself, that is, reason, does it? Would you know that you possessed reason by any other means than perceiving it by reason?

E.   This is most true.

37   *A*.   Then, when we perceive color, we do not likewise perceive that we perceive it by the sense of sight itself; when we hear a sound, we do not hear our own hearing; when we smell a rose, something has fragrance for us, but not our sense of smell. When we taste something, the sense of taste itself does not taste in our mouth. We touch something, but we cannot touch the sense of touch itself. Since this is so, it is clear that these five senses cannot perceive themselves, although all corporeal objects may be perceived by them.

E.   Yes.

IV.
The inner sense perceives that it perceives; the bodily senses do not.

38   *A*.   It is also clear, I think, not only that the inner sense perceives what is presented by the five senses of the body, but also that it perceives the bodily senses themselves. Otherwise,

a beast would not move either to seek or to avoid something,
unless the beast were aware that it perceived—a thing not perceived by any of the five senses. It is not so that it may know
(which is the function of reason) that a beast perceives that
it perceives, but only so that it may move. If this is still ob-   39
scure, it will become clearer if you turn your attention to one
sense, like sight, which will furnish a quite sufficient example.
A beast could not open its eye and move it to look at what it
wanted to see unless when the eye was closed, or when it
was not moved, the beast perceived that its eye did not see.
Moreover, if a beast is aware that it does not see when it does
not see, it is also aware that it sees when it sees; for when the
beast sees, it does not move its eye because of the same im-
pulse which causes it to move its eye when it does not see;
and it notes that it perceives both of these conditions.
Whether this life which is aware that it perceives corporeal   40
objects also perceives itself is not so obvious, unless we consider the fact that everyone, when he seeks within himself,
finds that every living thing avoids death. Since death is the
opposite of life, necessarily life, which avoids its opposite,
perceives itself. But if this is not yet clear, let us omit it, so   41
that we may work toward what we want only by clear, proven
evidence. This much is proven: corporeal objects are perceived by the senses of the body; a sense cannot perceive itself; moreover, by means of the inner sense, corporeal objects
are perceived through the senses of the body, and the senses
of the body themselves are also perceived by the inner sense;
but by means of reason, all these things, and reason itself,
become known and are included in knowledge. Do you not
think so?

    E.   I do indeed.

    A.   Now tell me: how stands the question toward whose
solution we have been struggling for so long upon this road?

V.
The inner sense that controls and judges the bodily senses is more excellent than the bodily senses.

42   *E.*   As I remember, of the three questions that we proposed to form the order of this discourse a little while ago, we are now dealing with the first: how we can prove that God exists, even though we believe it firmly and steadfastly.

A.   Your memory is correct. I also want you to keep carefully in mind that when I asked whether you knew you existed, it became obvious that you knew not only this, but also two other things [that you live and that you understand].

E.   I remember this as well.

43   *A.*   Now see in which of these three belongs everything that the senses of the body perceive; that is, in which of these classes would you place whatever reaches our senses through the eyes (or, for that matter, any organ of the body whatsoever)? In that which merely exists, that which also lives, or that which understands?

E.   In that which merely exists.

A.   In which class would you place the sense itself?

E.   In that which lives.

A.   Which of these two do you judge to be the better, the sense or its object?

E.   The sense, of course.

A.   Why?

E.   Because what lives is better than what merely exists.

44   *A.*   What of the inner sense, which we investigated previously and found to be inferior to reason, yet common to man and beast? Will you hesitate to rank this higher than the senses of the body—which, in turn, are to be ranked higher than the body itself?

E.   No, I would not.

45   *A.*   I would like to hear why you would not. You cannot say that the inner sense should be placed in that one of the three classes which understands as well, but only in that

which is or lives, since it lacks understanding; for the inner
sense is present in beasts as well, and they do not have understanding. Since this is so, I ask you why you place the inner
sense higher than the sense which perceives corporeal objects.
Both belong to the class that lives. Moreover, you placed the   46
sense that touches bodies over the bodies themselves, because
bodies are in the class of things that merely exist, while this
sense is in the class of things that live. Since the inner sense is
also found in the class that lives, tell me why you think it
better. If you say, "Because the inner sense perceives the
bodily sense," I believe that you will not find a rule by which
we can confidently assert that everything which perceives is
better than what it perceives. For by this same rule, we would
be forced to admit that everything which understands is
better than what is understood. This is false; for man under-   47
stands wisdom, yet he is not better than wisdom itself. Therefore, why do you think that the inner sense is to be placed
above the sense by which we perceive bodies?

   E.   Because I recognize that it controls and, as it were,   48
judges the bodily senses. If something is missing in the performance of their function, the inner sense demands its debt,
so to speak, from its servants, just as we proved a little while
ago. For the sense of the eye does not see that it sees or does
not see. Since it does not, it cannot judge what is missing or
what is sufficient. The inner sense, however, advises the bodily
sense, in the soul of a beast, to open the closed eyes and to
complete what it perceives is lacking. No one can doubt that
what judges is better than what is judged.

   A.   You assert, then, that the bodily sense makes judg-   49
ments in the same way about bodies? For pleasure and pain
affect the bodily sense when it is touched gently or roughly
by a body. Just as the inner sense judges what is lacking or
what is sufficient in the sense of the eyes, so the sense of the
eyes itself judges what is lacking or sufficient in color. Just as
the inner sense judges whether or not our hearing is intent
enough, so hearing itself judges voices, what flows in harmoni-
ously or what makes a harsh noise. We need not continue with   50

the rest of the senses. I think that you know what I mean: just as the inner sense makes judgments about the senses of the body, approving their completeness or demanding what is lacking, so the senses of the body make judgments about bodies, accepting from among them what is pleasing and rejecting what is not.

E.   I understand and agree.

VI.
Reason is the highest and most excellent faculty of man. God and that which is more excellent than reason.

51   A.   Now see if reason makes any judgment about the inner sense. I am not asking whether you doubt that reason is better than the inner sense, since I am sure you think it is. I think that now we do not need to question whether reason makes judgments about the inner sense. For, of the things that are under the reason—bodies, bodily senses, and the inner sense—how would one be better than another and reason more excellent than all, unless reason itself told us so? Certainly this is possible only if reason makes judgments concerning them.

E.   That is evident.

52   A.   Therefore, since the nature which merely exists and does not live or understand (for example, the inanimate body) is inferior to the nature that not only exists, but also lives, though it does not understand (for example, the soul of beasts); and since this in turn is inferior to that which at once exists, lives, and understands (for example, the rational mind in man)—you do not think then, do you, that anything can be found in us more excellent (that is, among those things by which our nature is perfected so that we are men) than this

53   which we put in the third place? Clearly we have a body, and a kind of life that makes the body live and grow. We recognize these two conditions in beasts as well. We have also a third thing: a head or eye of our soul, as it were, or whatever

term can be more aptly applied to our reason and understanding. This is what the nature of a beast does not have.
Please see whether you can find anything in man's nature
which is more noble than reason.

E.   I see absolutely nothing more noble.

A.   What if we should be able to find something which   54
you would not doubt not only exists, but even is more excellent than our reason? Will you hesitate to say that, whatever
it is, this is our God?

E.   If I could find something better than what is best in
my nature, I would not immediately say that this is God. I
am not inclined to call God that to which my reason is inferior, but rather that to whom no one is superior.

A.   Clearly. And God Himself has given your reason the   55
power to think so devoutly and truly about Him. But, I ask
you, if you find that there is nothing superior to our reason
except what is eternal and immutable, will you hesitate to say
that this is God? You know that bodies are mutable and that
life itself, which animates the body in its varying conditions,
is plainly subject to change. Reason itself is clearly proven to
be mutable, now struggling to arrive at truth, now ceasing to
struggle, sometimes reaching it and sometimes not. If, without   56
the aid of any organ of the body or of any sense inferior to it,
either touch, taste, smell, hearing, or sight, reason discerns that
it is inferior and through its own power discerns something
eternal and immutable, reason should at the same time admit
that it is inferior and that this is its God.

E.   I shall admit that this is God to which nothing is
granted to be superior.

A.   Good! It will be sufficient, then, for me to prove that   57
there is something of this nature which you will admit to be
God; or, if there is anything superior, you will grant that this
superior being is God. Therefore, whether there is something
superior or not, it will be proven that God exists when, as I
promised, I show with God's aid that there is something
superior to reason.

E.   Prove then what you promise.

VII.
How can the same object be known by many at the same time?

58   *A.*   I will. Let me ask first whether my bodily sense is the same as yours; or whether it is not really my sense, unless it be mine, and not really your sense, unless it be your own. Were it not so, I could not see through my eyes any object that you did not see.

59   *E.*   I admit this fully. Although senses are the same in kind, we each have our own senses of seeing, hearing, and so forth. Not only can one man see or hear what another cannot; but it is also possible for any person to perceive with any sense what someone else does not perceive. Thus it is proven that a sense is not yours unless it is yours, nor mine unless it is mine.

60   *A.*   Would you say the same thing about the inner sense, or something else?

    E.   The same, surely. My inner sense perceives my senses, and yours perceives yours. For this reason, I am often asked by a man who sees something whether I see it too. For I perceive whether or not I see it; he who asks does not perceive whether or not I see it.

61   *A.*   Well, does not each one of us have his own reason? For it can happen that I understand something which you do not understand and which you cannot know whether or not I understand, while I, on the other hand, do know that I understand it.

    E.   It is evident that each of us has his own rational mind.

62   *A.*   You could not say, could you, that each of us has his own sun, moon, stars, and so forth, which we see, although each perceives these with his own sense?

    E.   Of course not!

63   *A.*   Many of us at the same time can see some one object. Yet each of us has his own senses, with which each per-

ceives the one object that we all see simultaneously. Although my sense is different from yours, what we see is not necessarily mine or yours. One object is before both of us and is viewed by both of us at the same time.

E. That is very evident.

A. We can hear another voice at the same time; yet my hearing is distinct from yours, and the voice that we hear is neither mine nor yours. Whatever sound occurs is present in its entirety, to be heard by both of us. 64

E. This is also evident.

A. Now, please, turn your attention to what we say about the other senses of the body. They do not behave exactly as do the senses of the eyes or ears, because they have contact with the object; nor is their behavior entirely different. Both you and I can inhale the same air, and can perceive the character of this air from its odor. Likewise, we can both taste the same honey, or whatever food or drink you please, and we can perceive its character from its taste. Although the air or honey is the same, and although the odor or taste is the same when we both experience it, nevertheless you do not experience it with my sense, nor I with yours, nor do we experience it with some other sense which both of us possess in common. My sense is my own and yours is your own, even though the odor or taste experienced by both of us is the same. From the above reasoning, these senses are found to be something like the senses of sight and hearing. But for the purposes of our discussion, they differ from sight and hearing in the following way: both of us draw in the same air through our noses and taste the same food; nevertheless, I do not breathe that part of the air that you breathe and I do not take the same part of the food that you take. Each of us takes a different part. When I take a breath from the whole air, I take in the part which is sufficient for me, and you likewise breathe from the whole air the part which is sufficient for you. And although a certain food is completely consumed by both of us, nevertheless not all is consumed by you or by me, in the same way that we both at the same time 65 66 67 68

hear a whole word or see the same sight. Different parts of the
food or drink must enter each of us. Do you understand this?

E.   I agree that this is clear and true.

69   A.   You don't think, do you, that the sense of touch can
be compared to the sense of the eyes and ears in the case we
have just discussed? Not only can both of us perceive one
body through the sense of touch, but even the same part of a
70   body. This is not the case when we are both eating; we cannot both take all of the food placed before us, as, with the
sense of touch, you could touch the same object that I
touched, and all of it—so that both of us each touched, not
just individual parts of the object, but the whole object.

71   E.   I admit that in this way the sense of touch is very
like the sense of seeing and hearing. But I see a difference:
both of us can see and hear one entire object at the same
time. Both of us, however, cannot touch an entire object at
one time, only a part at a time; and not the same part, except
at different times. I cannot touch any part that you are touch-
ing unless you move away from it.

72   A.   A most acute answer! Yet attend to this: of all the
objects that we perceive, there are some which both of us perceive at the same time and others which we each perceive
separately. Yet each of us perceives his own sensations separately; I never feel yours and you never feel mine. What can
each of us separately, not both together, perceive from among
those things that are perceived by us through the bodily
senses, that is, from among corporeal objects, except what
becomes our own so completely that we change it into our-
73   selves? For instance, food and drink. You cannot perceive any
part of food or drink that I have perceived. Even though
nurses give infants food that has already been chewed, the
part that has already been tasted, chewed, and absorbed
into the vitals of the one who chewed it cannot in any way
74   be called back as food for the infant. When the palate has
tasted something pleasant, however small that part may be,
the palate claims it irrevocably as its own and forces it to conform to the nature of the body. Were this not so, there would
remain no taste in the mouth after the food which was bitten

off and tasted has been spit out. The same can also be said of 75
the parts of the air that we inhale through the nose. Although
you too can inhale all that I have exhaled, you cannot breathe
in what has been used as nourishment because I cannot ex-
hale that part. Doctors teach us that we take in nourishment
through our nose. This nourishment I alone can perceive by
inhaling, and I cannot restore it by exhaling for you to inhale
and perceive through your nose. When we perceive other 76
sorts of sensible objects we do not, in the act of perception,
break them up and absorb them into our body. Both of us
can perceive them either at one time or separately, so that
either all or part of what I perceive may also be perceived
by you. Examples of this are light, sound, or corporeal bodies,
with which we come into contact but, in so doing, do not
alter them.

E.   I understand.

A.   It is, therefore, clear that objects we do not change 77
when we perceive them with our bodily senses do not become
part of the nature of our senses and so are common to us,
since they are not changed or turned into our own, as it were,
personal property.

E.   I agree completely.

A.   By "our own" and "personal," I mean that which 78
each one of us consumes for himself and what each alone perceives in himself as belonging properly to his own nature.
By "common" and, as it were, "public," I mean what is perceived by everyone who perceives, without its being changed
or destroyed.

E.   Yes.

VIII.
The order of numbers, known as one and unchangeable, is not known by the bodily senses.

A.   Come! Listen and tell me whether we may find any- 79
thing that all reasoning men see with their reason and mind
in common with all others, while what is seen is present in all

and, unlike food or drink, is not transformed into some use by those to whom it is present, instead remaining uncorrupted and complete whether or not men discern it. Perhaps you think that nothing like this exists?

80   E.   On the contrary, I see that many such things exist, one of which is quite enough to mention: the order and the truth of number [*ratio et veritas numeri*] are present to all who think. Everyone who calculates tries to understand the truth of number with his own reason and understanding. Some can do this rather easily; others have more difficulty. Yet the truth of number offers itself to all alike who are able to grasp it. When a man understands it, it is not changed into a kind of nourishment for him; when he fails to grasp it, the truth of number does not disappear; rather, it remains true and permanent, while man's failure to grasp it is commensurate with the extent of his error.

81   A.   Correct! I see that you are not inexperienced in this, and have quickly found your answer. If someone were to say to you that numbers were impressed upon our spirit not as a result of their own nature, but as a result of those objects which we experience with the bodily senses, what answer would you make? Or do you agree with this?

82   E.   No, I do not. Even if I did perceive numbers with the bodily senses, I would not be able to perceive with the bodily senses the meaning of division and addition. It is with the light of the mind that I would prove wrong the man who makes an error in addition or subtraction. Whatever I may experience with my bodily senses, such as this air and earth and whatever corporeal matter they contain, I cannot know

83   how long it will endure. But seven and three are ten, not only now, but forever. There has never been a time when seven and three were not ten, nor will there ever be a time when they are not ten. Therefore, I have said that the truth of number is incorruptible and common to all who think.

84   A.   I do not disagree with your answer, for you spoke truly and clearly. But you will easily see that numbers themselves are not drawn from the bodily senses, if you realize how

any number you please multiplied by one is that number.
For example, two times one is two; three times one is three;
ten times one is ten; any number times one is that number.
Anyone who really thinks about the number one realizes that   85
he cannot perceive it through the bodily senses, for whatever we experience through a sense is proven to be many, not
one. This follows because it is a body and is therefore infi-
nitely divisible. But I need not concentrate upon each small
and indistinct part; however small such a bodily part may
be, it has a right, left, upper, and lower side, or a farther and
nearer side, or ends and a middle. These, we admit, must   86
be in a body, however small it is; thus, we concede that no
body is truly and purely one. Yet all these parts could not be
counted, if they had not been distinguished by the concept
of one. When, therefore, I look for one in a body, I do not
doubt that I will not find it. I know what I am seeking there
and what I shall not find there. I know that I cannot find
one, or rather that it does not exist in a body at all. How do   87
I know that a body is not one? If I did not know what one is,
I could not count the many parts of the body. Moreover, however I may know one, I do not know it through the bodily
senses, because through the bodily senses I know nothing except
a body which, we have proven, is not really and simply one.
Furthermore, if we have not perceived one through a sense of
the body, we have not perceived by a sense any number of
those numbers which we discern only through the understanding. There exists no number which does not get its name   88
from the number of times it contains one. The perception of
one does not occur through any bodily sense. The half of any
body whatsoever, although the whole body consists of two
halves, also has its own half; therefore, there are two parts of
a body which are not simply two. Moreover, the number
which is called two because it is twice what is irreducibly one,
cannot be two parts of one, in other words, that which is
simply one cannot again have a half or a third or whatever
part you please, since it is simply and truly one. In observing   89
the order of numbers, we see after one the number two, which

is twice one. Twice two does not follow next in order; rather,
90 three comes next, and then four, which is twice two. This
order [*ratio*] continues throughout all the rest of the numbers
by a fixed and unchangeable law. Thus after one, the first of
all numbers, when one itself is excepted, the first number is
the double of one, for two comes next. After this second
number, that is, after two, when two is excepted, the second
number is the double of two; for after two the first number is three, and the second number is four, the double of
two. After the third, that is, after the number three, when it
is itself excepted, the third number is the double of three; for
after the third number, that is, after three, the first number
is four, the second five, and the third six, which is the double
91 of three. So after the fourth number, when it is itself excepted, the fourth number is the double of four; for after
the fourth number, after four, the first number is five, the
second is six, the third is seven, and the fourth number is
eight, which is the double of four. Through all of the rest of
the numbers you will find the same thing that is found in the
first pair of numbers, one and two, namely, the double of any
number is as many times after this number as such a number
is from the beginning.

92 How do we discern that this fact which holds for the whole
number series is unchangeable, fixed, and incorruptible? No
one perceives all the numbers by any bodily sense, for they are
innumerable. How do we know that this is true for all numbers? Through what fantasy or vision do we discern so confidently the firm truth of number throughout the whole innumerable series, unless by some inner light unknown to
bodily sense?

93 Men to whom God has given ability in argument, and
whom stubbornness does not lead into confusion, are forced
to admit that the order and truth of numbers have nothing
to do with the bodily senses, but are unchangeable and true
94 and common to all rational beings. Therefore, although many
other things could occur to us that are common and, as it
were, public for rational beings, things that are seen by each

individual with his mind and reason and still remain inviolate and unchanged, nevertheless, I am not unwilling to accept the fact that the order and truth of number are the best possible examples that you could have given when you wished to answer my question. Not without reason was number joined 95 to wisdom in the Holy Scriptures where it is said, "I and my heart have gone round to know and to consider and to search out wisdom and number." [1]

IX.
Is wisdom, which is necessary for human happiness, one and the same in all men who are wise?

A. Nevertheless, I beg you, what opinion should we 96 have in the case of wisdom itself? Do you think that each man has his own individual wisdom? Or is there one wisdom that exists alike for all men, such that the more a man partakes of this wisdom, the wiser he is?

E. I do not know what wisdom you mean. I see that 97 men have various opinions as to what is said or done wisely. Men who serve as soldiers think that they are acting wisely, while men who despise military service, devoting their energy and effort to agriculture, praise agriculture and claim that this is wisdom. Men who are shrewd in devising ways of acquiring wealth think that they are wise. Men who disregard all this or put aside temporal things of this sort, devoting their whole effort to the search for truth so that they may know themselves and God—these men judge that this is the great gift of wisdom. Those who are not willing to devote 98 themselves to the leisure of seeking and contemplating truth, but prefer toilsome business and official duties so that they may advise men and engage in the just government and management of human affairs—these men think that they are wise. Men who do both of these things and live some of the time in the contemplation of truth, and some of the time amid toilsome official duties which they think they owe to human

[1] Eccles. 7:26 (Eccles. 7:25).

99 society, think that they hold the prize of wisdom. I pass over innumerable sects, all of which rank their own followers over others and claim that they alone are wise. Therefore, since we are discussing the problem between us in such a way that we must assert, not our beliefs, but only what we clearly understand, I cannot answer your question unless I know by reflection and reasoning what wisdom itself is.

100   *A.*   You don't think, do you, that wisdom is anything other than the truth in which the highest good is discerned and held? All the different sects that you mentioned seek good and avoid evil. Their doctrines vary because different things appear to them to be good. Whoever, then, seeks what he should not seek, errs, even though he would not seek it if he did not think it good. The man who seeks nothing cannot

101 err, nor can the man who seeks what he ought to seek. Insofar as all men seek the happy life, they do not err. Insofar as each man fails to follow the road of life that leads to happiness, although he may confess and profess that he is unwilling to arrive anywhere except at happiness, he is in error. His error is that he follows something that does not

102 lead where he wishes to arrive. The greater his error on the road of life, the less his wisdom, and the farther he is from the truth in which the highest good is discerned and grasped. Moreover, when the highest good has been pursued and obtained, each man becomes happy—which beyond a doubt is what we all wish. Just as it is agreed that we all wish to be happy, so it is agreed that we all wish to be wise, since no one without wisdom is happy. No man is happy except through the highest good, which is to be found and included

103 in that truth which we call wisdom. Just as the idea of happiness is impressed upon our minds before we are happy— through this idea we know confidently and say without hesitation that we wish to be happy—so, before we are wise, we have an idea of wisdom in our minds. Through this idea each one of us, if asked whether or not he wants to be wise, answers without any confusion or doubt that he does so wish.

104   If it is, therefore, agreed between us what wisdom is, al-

though perhaps you could not explain wisdom in words—for if you did not discern wisdom at all with your spirit, you would not know either that you wish to be wise or that you ought to wish to be wise, which I do not think you will deny —I want you to tell me whether you think that wisdom offers itself alike to all who think, just as the order and truth of number do. Or since there are as many minds as there are men, so that I discern nothing in your mind and you discern nothing in mine, do you think that there can be as many wisdoms as there are wise men?

E.   If the highest good is one for all men, the truth in   105 which it is discerned and grasped—that is, wisdom—must be one and common to all men.

A.   Do you doubt that the highest good, whatever it is, is one for all men?

E.   Yes, I do, because I see different men rejoicing in different things as their highest goods.

A.   Indeed, I wish that no one had any doubt about   106 the highest good, just as no one has any doubt that a man cannot be happy without obtaining the highest good. Since the question is important, and may demand a long explanation, let us imagine that the highest goods are as many as the different things which are sought by various men as the highest good. It does not follow, does it, that wisdom itself is not common alike to all men, just because the goods which men discern in it and choose are many and varied? If you   107 think this, you may also doubt that the light of the sun is one, because we see many different things in it. From these many things, each man chooses according to his will what he may enjoy through his sight. One man willingly looks at the height of a mountain and rejoices to see it; another at the level fields; another at the hollow of valleys; another at the greenness of the woods; another at the flickering surface of the sea; another compares all or some of these things at the same time, for the delight of seeing them. Just as the objects   108 which men see in the sunlight and choose to enjoy are many and varied, yet the light in which the sight of each man

watching sees and holds what he enjoys is one; so even if the
goods are many and varied from which each man may choose
what he wishes, determining to discern, grasp, and enjoy the
highest good rightly and truly, nevertheless it is possible that
the very light of wisdom, in which these goods can be discerned and grasped, is one wisdom common to all wise men.

109   *E.*   I grant that this can be so and that nothing is opposed to the existence of one wisdom common to all, even if
there are many different highest goods. But I would like to
know whether or not this is so; for when we grant that this
may possibly be so, we do not necessarily grant that it *is* so.

A.   Meanwhile, we maintain that wisdom exists. But
whether it is one and common to all men, or whether each
individual has his own wisdom as he has his own soul or
mind, we do not yet know.

E.   Yes.

X.
The rules of wisdom are the same for all wise men.

110   *A.*   How, then, do we see the truth of what we are maintaining: that wisdom and wise men exist, and that all men
wish to be happy? I do not doubt that you see this and see
that it is true. Do you see that this is true in the same way
that you see your own thoughts, of which I am completely
ignorant, unless you disclose them to me? Or do you see it
in the same way that you understand, that is, in such a way
that I too can see the truth, even though you do not disclose
it to me?

111   *E.*   I do not doubt that you can see the truth also, even
though I might not want you to.

A.   Is not the one truth which we both see in our individual minds common to both of us?

E.   Clearly.

A.   Likewise, I believe, you do not deny the truth that
we should seek after wisdom.

E.   I do not doubt it.

A.   Can we deny that this fact is true and one, yet com-   112
mon for all who know it? Each man sees it with his own mind,
not with mine, yours, or anyone else's; yet what is seen, is
present for all to see in common. We cannot deny this, can
we?

E.   Of course not.

A.   Won't you also admit the following to be absolutely   113
true: that we should live justly; that the worse should be subordinate to the better; that equals should be compared with
equals and to each should be given his own; and that each of
these truths is present for you, me, and all to see in common?

E.   Yes.

A.   Will you deny that the incorrupt is better than the   114
corrupt, the eternal better than the temporal, the inviolable
better than the violable?

E.   Who can deny this?

A.   Can anyone call truth his own, when it is present
unchangingly, for all to meditate upon who have the power
to meditate?

E.   No one can truly call truth his own. Truth is one
and common to all, just as much as it is true.

A.   Likewise, who can deny that the spirit should be   115
turned away from corruption and toward incorruption, and
that incorruption, not corruption, should be loved? When a
man grants something to be true, does he not also understand that it is changeless, and does he not see that it is present in common for all minds that have the power to behold
it?

E.   True.

A.   Will anyone doubt that the life which cannot be
moved by any opposition from a sure and honest judgment
is better than the one which is easily broken and overcome
by the troubles of this life?

E.   Who would doubt it?

A.   I shall not ask any more questions of this kind. It   116
is sufficient that you see and grant, as I do, that it is certain
that these judgments are rules and, as it were, lights of vir-

tue; and that true and unchangeable things, whether individually or all together, are present in common for all men to meditate upon who have the power to perceive with mind and reason. I do ask this however: Do you think that these things are a part of wisdom? I believe that you think that the man who has gained wisdom is wise.

117   E.   Yes.

A.   Could a man who lives justly live this way if he did not see which are the inferior things that he subordinates to superior ones, or the equals that he joins to equals, or the particular things that he assigns to their own particular places?

E.   He could not.

A.   You won't deny, will you, that the man who sees these things sees wisely?

E.   No.

A.   Likewise, doesn't the man who lives prudently choose incorruption and judge that incorruption is to be preferred to corruption?

E.   Most clearly.

A.   Therefore, when he chooses to turn his spirit to that which no one doubts should be chosen, it cannot be denied, can it, that he chooses wisely?

E.   Of course not.

A.   When, therefore, he turns his mind to a wise choice, he does so wisely.

E.   Certainly.

A.   And he acts wisely who is not turned by fear or punishment from what he chooses or turns to wisely.

E.   Without a doubt.

118   A.   It is very clear, then, that all that we have called the rules and lights to virtue are a part of wisdom, inasmuch as the more a man uses them in leading his life, the more wisely he acts and lives. Moreover, whatever is done wisely cannot rightly be said to be separate from wisdom.

E.   Yes.

119   A.   The true and immutable rules of wisdom are as true

and immutable as the rules of number, whose order and truth, you have said, are unchangeably present and common to all who see them. When asked about a few of these rules of wisdom individually, you replied that they were evidently true, and you admitted that they are present and common for all to see who have the power to see them.

XI.
How are the rules of number and wisdom related?

E. I cannot doubt this. But I would very much like to know whether these two things, wisdom and number, are members of any single class. You recall that they have been placed together in the Holy Scriptures. Does one depend on the other, or is the one included in the other? Does number, for example, depend upon wisdom, or is it included in wisdom? I do not dare to say that wisdom depends upon number, or is included in number; this could hardly be the case, since I have known many accountants and men skilled in numbers (whatever name is applied to men who use numbers well and accurately), yet I have known few wise men—perhaps none. Wisdom seems by far more worthy than number. 120

A. You have mentioned something at which I too often wonder. When I think about the unchanging truth of numbers, and when I consider the province of numbers—their room or sanctuary, as it were, or whatever suitable name can be found by which we may designate the home or seat of numbers—I am far removed from my body. I may, perhaps, find something about which I can think, but it is nothing that I can express in words; as though exhausted, I return to familiar things, so as to be able to speak, and I speak of objects before my eyes, objects that it is usual to speak of. The same thing happens to me when I think as carefully and intently as I can about wisdom. Besides, I am very much amazed because these two things lie in the most secret and yet most certain truth—even by the testimony of the Scriptures, where number and wisdom are placed together. I won- 122 123

der greatly, as I said before, why number is generally regarded as of little value while wisdom is thought precious.
Yet number and wisdom are somehow one and the same thing,
124 since the Divine Writings say of wisdom that it "reaches from
end to end powerfully and disposes all things sweetly." [1] The
power that "reaches from end to end powerfully" is perhaps
called "number"; while the power which "disposes all things
sweetly" is now thought of as wisdom proper, though both
125 of these belong to the same wisdom. Because wisdom gave
numbers to all objects, even the lowliest objects that have
been placed at the very end; because all objects, even the least
ones, have their own numbers; because, moreover, wisdom did
not grant, either to corporeal objects or to all spirits, the
power to know, but granted it only to rational beings, as if
it made in them a home for itself, from which it could arrange everything, including even the least object to which it
has assigned number; because we easily make judgments about
corporeal objects as things which have been placed in a lower
order than ours and which we see are beneath us, even though
numbers has been stamped upon them—for these reasons, we
consider these numbers to be inferior to ourselves and therefore regard them as baser.

126   But when we begin, as it were, to ascend along the path,
we discover that numbers transcend our minds and remain
unchangeable in their own truth. Because few men can know,
but even stupid men can count, men admire wisdom and despise numbers. Yet the further removed learned students are
from the filth of the earth, the more clearly do they apprehend both numbers and wisdom in truth itself, and they
hold both of them to be precious. For them, not only do
silver, gold, and the other things for which we strive bear no
comparison with this truth, but even they themselves appear
127 worthless when compared to it. Therefore, do not marvel
that, while wisdom has appeared precious to men, number has
seemed base: it has seemed so because men can count more easily

1 Wisd. of Sol. 8:1.

BOOK TWO

than they can know. You see that men consider gold more precious than the golden light of a lamp, in comparison with which gold is to be scorned. Yet the lesser object receives more honor because even a beggar may light a lamp for himself, while few men have gold. The comparison suggests that wisdom, since it is rare, is inferior to number—which is impossible, since they are identical; but it requires an eye capable of discerning it. Brightness and heat are perceived consubstantially, so 128 to speak, in the one fire; they cannot be separated. Yet the heat is communicated to objects which are placed near to the fire, while brightness is diffused far and wide. In the same way, the power of intelligence, which lies in wisdom, warms things (such as rational souls) that lie near it. But the power of intelligence does not affect things that are farther away, (for instance, corporeal objects) with the heat of knowing; it floods them, rather, with the light of numbers. This com- 129 parison may be somewhat obscure to you, for no analogy from visible things can be made applicable in every respect to that which is invisible.

Yet attend to the following point which is sufficient for our question and is clear enough, even to humble minds like ours. Although it is not clear to us whether number is a part of or separate from wisdom, or whether wisdom is a part of or separate from number, or whether they are the same, it is clear that both are true, and immutably true.

XII.
One immutable truth, common to all who know, exists, and is more excellent than the minds that know it.

A.   You will not deny, therefore, that immutable truth, 130 comprising everything that is immutably true, exists; and you cannot say that immutable truth is yours, or mine, or anyone else's. It is present and shows itself as a kind of miraculously secret, yet public, light for all who see what is im-

131 mutably true. Who would say, then, that anything which is present for all who think and know belongs exclusively to the nature of any one of these?

You remember, I imagine, that we have already given some discussion to the senses of the body. The objects which we perceive in common by means of the sense of the eyes or ears —colors and sounds, for example, which you and I can see and hear at the same time—these objects do not belong to the nature of our eyes or ears, but are common for both of 132 us to perceive. You will not, therefore, say that the objects which you and I perceive together, each with our own mind, belong to the natures of either of us. We cannot say that the object seen by the eyes of two people belongs to either of the two. It is, instead, some third object, upon which the sight of each of the two is directed.

E.   This is evidently the case.

133 *A.*   Do you think that the truth of which we have been talking for so long, and in which, though it is one, we see so many things—do you think that this truth is more excellent than our minds, or equally so, or less? If it were less excellent, we would make judgments *about* it, not *according to* it. In the same way, we make judgments about corporeal objects because they are below us, and we say not only that they are or are not this way, but also that they ought to be this way, or ought not to be. It is likewise concerning our spirits: we know not only that the spirit *is,* but often also that it *ought* 134 *to be,* such and such. When we speak about corporeal objects, we make the following judgments: this is less bright than it should be; or, it is not so square; and so forth. We speak, however, the following way, according to the nature of our character [*morum ratio*], about spirits: this is less apt than it ought to be; or, less gentle; or, less forceful. We make these judgments according to the inner rules of truth which we perceive in common. But no one makes judgments about the rules themselves. When a man says that the eternal is more powerful than the temporal, and that seven plus three are ten, he does not say that it ought to be so; he knows it

is this way, and does not correct it as an examiner would, but he rejoices as if he has made a discovery.

If truth were equal to our minds, it would be subject to 135
change. Our minds sometimes see more and sometimes less, and because of this we acknowledge that they are mutable. Truth, remaining in itself, does not gain anything when we see it, or lose anything when we do not see it. It is whole and uncorrupted. With its light, truth gives joy to the men who turn to it, and punishes with blindness those who turn away from it.

What of the fact that in accordance with truth we make 136
judgments about our minds, yet we cannot make judgments about the truth? We say that a mind knows less than it ought to, or as much as it should. Moreover, the nearer the mind can get to immutable truth and the more closely it can cling to the truth, the more the mind ought to know. Therefore, if truth is neither inferior nor equal to our minds, it follows that it is superior to them, and more excellent.

XIII.
Man's enjoyment of the truth.

A.   But I promised, if you remember, that I would show 137
you something higher than our mind and reason. Behold, it is truth itself. If you can, embrace it, enjoy it; "Be glad in the Lord, and He will grant you the prayers of your heart." [1]
What more do you ask than that you be happy? And what is more blessed than the man who enjoys unshaken, immutable, and most excellent truth? Men declare that they are happy 138
when they embrace beautiful bodies that they have ardently desired, whether of their wives or of prostitutes; do we doubt that we are happy in the embrace of truth? Men exclaim how happy they are when, with throats parched from the heat, they come to a flowing and healthful spring; or when they are hungry and find a plentiful supper or dinner prepared. Shall we deny that we are happy when we are given

[1] Ps. 36:4 (Ps. 37:4).

139   the food and drink of truth? We usually hear voices of men declaring that they are happy if they rest among roses and other flowers or if they enjoy fragrant perfumes. What is more fragrant or more pleasant than the breath of truth? Do we hesitate to say that we are happy when we breathe the truth? Many think that the life lived amid the music of voice, stringed instrument, or flute is happy, and when they lack this, they think themselves unhappy; when they have it, they are elated with joy. Do we ask for any other happy life, when, so to speak, the silent eloquence of truth glides noiselessly into our minds? Do we not then enjoy a happiness that is

140   sure, and near at hand? Men think themselves happy and want to live forever when they are delighted by the brightness of gold, silver, gems, colors; or by the light of their eyes themselves; or by the fires of the earth, the stars, the moon, or the sun. They are delighted by brightness and joy, as long as trouble or poverty do not separate them from this happiness. Are we afraid to place the happy life in the light of truth?

141   Furthermore, because the highest good is known and grasped by truth, and because this truth is wisdom, let us, by our wisdom, see and grasp the highest good, and enjoy it. Happy indeed is the man who enjoys the highest good. It is this truth that reveals all true goods, and every man in accordance with his capacity chooses them, either individually

142   or together, for his enjoyment. Men choose by the light of the sun what they wish to see, and they rejoice in the sight. If they are by chance endowed with strong, keen, and healthy eyes, they look at nothing more willingly than at the sun which lights up even the other things by which men with weak eyes are delighted. In the same way, when the rapier edge of the mind cuts through the many true and immutable things with its sure reason, it steers toward the very truth, by which all things are revealed; clinging to truth as if forgetful of all else, it enjoys everything at once in its enjoyment of truth. Whatever is delightful in other truths derives its delightfulness from truth itself.

Our freedom then consists in submission to the truth. It 143
is our God Himself who frees us from death, that is, from the
state of sin. Truth itself, when it speaks as a man, says to
those who believe in Him, "If you remain in My word, you
shall be My disciples indeed, and you shall know the truth
and the truth will make you free." [2] The soul enjoys nothing
with freedom, unless it enjoys it securely.

XIV.
Truth, available in common to all men, is the private property of no man.

A.   No one, however, securely possesses those goods 144
which he can lose although he does not wish to. And no one
can lose truth and wisdom against his will, for no one can be
physically separated from them. That which is called separa-
tion from truth and wisdom is the perverse will which loves
inferior things. No one wills a thing unwillingly. We possess 145
in the truth, therefore, what we all may enjoy, equally and in
common; in it are no defects or limitations. For truth receives
all its lovers without arousing their envy. It is open to all,
yet it is always chaste. No one says to the other, "Get back!
Let me approach too! Hands off! Let me also embrace it!"
All men cling to truth, and touch it. The food of truth can 146
never be stolen. There is nothing that you can drink of it
which I cannot drink too. You do not turn anything to your
private advantage by communion with truth. Whatever you
may take from truth and wisdom, they still remain complete
for me. I need not wait for you to return the source of your
inspiration in order that I too can be inspired by truth. No
part of truth is ever made the private property of anyone;
rather, it is entirely common to all at the same time. The ob- 147
jects, therefore, that we touch, taste, or smell, are less like
truth than are the things we see and hear. This is because
every word is heard in its entirety by all who hear it, and at

2 John 8:31–32.

the same time by each individual; and every sight which lies before the eyes is seen as much by one individual as by another at the same time.

148   There is, however, a very great difference despite these similarities. No voice whatsoever sounds in its entirety at one time, for it is extended and produced in time so that one part sounds earlier and another later. Also, every visible sight swells out, as it were, in space, and is not complete in any one spot. These objects may all be taken away although we may not want them to be, and we are prevented by certain limita-
149   tions from being able to enjoy them. If someone's sweet singing could be eternal, men would come eagerly in crowds to hear him; the larger the crowd, the more each would fight for a place nearer to the singer. In hearing him, they could retain nothing permanent, but would be touched by fleeting
150   notes. Moreover, if I wished to look upon the sun and could do so continuously, it would only leave me at sunset or be veiled by a cloud, and I would, though unwillingly, lose the pleasure of seeing the sun because of the many obstacles. Finally, if the sweetness of light or of sound were forever present for me to see or hear, what advantage would this be
151   to me, since I would share this in common with brutes? When the will to enjoy is continually present, the beauty of truth and wisdom does not shut out those who have come to hear because of the large crowd; it does not pass with time, and does not move in space. It is not cut short by night or shad-
152   ows. It does not depend on the senses of the body. It is near to all men who have chosen it and love it. It is eternal for all. It is in no one place, yet it is never away. Without, it advises; within, it teaches. It changes for the better all who behold it, and is not changed for the worse by anyone. No man passes judgment on truth, and no man judges well without it. For this reason it is clear that the beauty of truth and wisdom is, without doubt, superior to our minds, which become wise only through this beauty and which make judgments, not about it but through it, on other things.

XV.
God, that which is more excellent than reason, demonstrably exists.

A. You granted, moreover, that if I showed you something 153
higher than our minds, you would admit, assuming that nothing existed which was still higher, that God exists. I accepted
your condition and said that it was enough to show this. For
if there is something more excellent than truth, this is God.
If there is not, then truth itself is God. Whether or not truth
is God, you cannot deny that God exists, and this was the
question with which we agreed to deal. If it disturbs you that 154
we accept on faith that God is the "Father of Wisdom" in
the Sacred Teaching of Christ, remember that we also accept
on faith that wisdom born of the eternal is equal to the
Father. This is not the question at hand, but it is to be maintained with unshakable faith. For God exists, truly and in
the highest degree. This indubitable fact we maintain, I 155
think, not only by faith, but also by a sure though somewhat
tenuous form of reasoning, which is sufficient for the immediate question. Thus we can explain the other points perti-
nent to our discussion, unless you have some objection to raise
about the preceding parts.

E. I can scarcely find words for the unbelievable joy 156
that fills me. I accept these arguments, crying out that they
are most certain. And my inner voice shouts, for truth itself
to hear, that I cling to this: not only does good exist, but indeed the highest good—and this is the source of happiness.

A. Fine. I too am happy. But, I ask you, we are not 157
now wise and happy, are we? Rather, do we not strive toward
attaining this goal?

E. I think that we are striving toward the goal.

A. How do you understand that these are certain truths,
so that you cry out that you are happy? You admit that this
joy comes from wisdom. Can a foolish man know wisdom?

E.   Not so long as he is foolish.

158   *A.*   Then you are wise, or else you do not yet know wisdom.

E.   I am not yet wise, but I would not say that I am foolish insofar as I know wisdom, for I cannot deny that the things I know are certain, and that they belong to wisdom.

A.   Please tell me, don't you admit that the man who is not just is unjust? And he who is not prudent is imprudent? He who is not temperate is intemperate? Or do you have any doubts about this?

E.   I admit that, when a man is not just, he is unjust. I would also give the same answer in regard to the prudent or the temperate man.

159   *A.*   Why, then, is a man not foolish when he is not wise?

E.   I admit this too. When someone is not wise, he is foolish.

A.   Now which of these are you?

E.   Whichever you want to call me. I do not dare say that I am wise; and from what I have just admitted I must indubitably conclude that I am foolish.

160   *A.*   Therefore, the foolish man knows wisdom. As we have already said, he would not be sure that he wanted to be wise and that he ought to be wise, unless the idea of wisdom [*notio sapientiae*] was inherent in his mind. So it is with those individual things that belong to wisdom itself, about which I have just questioned you, and in the knowledge of which you rejoice.

E.   It is as you say.

XVI.
Wisdom shows itself to the seeker in the guise of numbers embodied in all things of this world.

161   *A.*   When we are eager to be wise, we simply, and as quickly as we can, find some means of concentrating our whole soul on the object; when it is attained by the mind, we fix it there firmly, not so that the soul may rejoice in its own

private pleasure—which involves only fleeting pleasures—but
so that the soul, free of all inclination toward the things of
time and space, may grasp that which is one, the same, and
eternal. As the soul is the whole life of the body, so God is 162
the happy life of the soul. This is the undertaking in which
we are engaged, and toward which we will strive until we
have completed it. It has been granted to us to enjoy these
true and certain goods which gleam before us, however obscured they may have been until this stage of our journey.
Is this not what was written of wisdom's treatment of its
lovers, when they approach and seek it? It is said, "In the
ways it will show itself to them joyfully and in all providence
it will meet them." [1] Wherever you turn, wisdom speaks to 163
you through the imprint it has stamped upon its works.
When you begin to slip toward outward things, wisdom calls
you back, by means of their very forms, so that when something delights you in body and entices you through the bodily
senses, you may see that it has number and may ask whence
it comes. Thus you return to yourself: you know that you cannot approve or disapprove of what you touch with the bodily
senses, unless you have within you certain laws of beauty to
which you refer the beautiful objects that you perceive outside of you.

Look at the sky, the earth, and the sea, and at whatever in 164
them shines from above or crawls, flies, or swims below. These
have form because they have number. Take away these forms
and there will be nothing. Whence are these except from
number? Indeed, they exist only insofar as they have number.

In art, the makers of all bodily forms have numbers by 165
which they organize their works. They move their hands and
instruments in producing their works until what has been
formed externally achieves completion by corresponding as
closely as possible to the inward light; and when it has been
communicated by the intermediaries of the senses, it delights
the inner judge who gazes upward upon numbers. Ask next
what moves the limbs of the artist himself, and it will be

[1] Wisd. of Sol. 6:17.

166   number, for his limbs also are moved according to number. If
you take the work from his hands and take the purpose of
creating the work from his spirit, and if you say that pleasure
causes the motion of the limbs, it will be called "dancing." If
you ask what is pleasant in dancing, number will answer you,
"Behold, it is I." Look closely at the beauty of the graceful
body and you will see that numbers are held in space. Then
look closely at the beauty of motion in a body and you will
see that numbers are involved in time. Enter into the art from
which the numbers come, and ask there for time and space.
Neither will exist; yet number lives there. Number has no
167   location in space [*regio spatiorum*], no duration of time. Nevertheless, when the men who wish to become artists adapt themselves to the art to be learned, they move their bodies through
time and space. They move their spirits through time; indeed,
their skill increases with the passage of time.

Go beyond even the spirit of an artist, that you may see
eternal number. Then wisdom will shine upon you from its
inner abode and from the shrine of truth. If your sight is still
too weak and is repelled from this vision, turn the eye of your
mind to the road where wisdom used to reveal itself for your
delight. Then remember that you have postponed a vision
which you may seek again when you are stronger and sounder.

168   Woe to men who forsake you as their leader, O Wisdom,
and wander from your footsteps! Woe to those who love not
you, but the signs you show, and who forget your meaning! O
sweetest light of the purified mind! Wisdom! You do not
cease to suggest to us what you are. Your beckoning is all the
beauty of creation.

By the very beauty of his work the artist somehow beckons
the spectator, instead of fixing his eyes wholly on the beauty
of the work he has made, to pass over this beauty and to look
in fondness at him who made it. In the same way, the men
169   who love not you, but what you make, are like those who hear
an eloquent wise man and, while they listen avidly to the
sweetness of his voice and the formation of his well-placed
syllables, lose what is most important—the meaning of the
ideas, of which the words were merely signs.

Woe to the men who turn from your light and cling com-
placently to their own darkness! When they turn their back
to you, they are fixed in the work of flesh, as in their own
shadows; yet even there, they receive what delights them
from the encompassing brightness of your light. But love of   170
the shadow causes the soul's eye to become too lazy and weak
to endure the splendor of the sight of you. Besides, the more
willingly and more indulgently a man follows and accepts
something very weak, the more he becomes covered with darkness, and gradually he becomes unable to see what is supreme.
He begins to think that some evil is deceiving him in his
blindness, or attracts him in his poverty, or has captured and
is torturing him. Yet he is really suffering deservedly because
he has turned from the light of wisdom; what is just cannot
be evil.

Therefore, Evodius, if you look at something mutable, you   171
cannot grasp it either with the bodily senses or the consideration of the mind, unless it possesses some numerical form. If
this form is removed, the mutable dissolves into nothing; do
not, then, doubt that there is some eternal and immutable
Form which prevents mutable objects from being destroyed
and allows them to complete their temporal course, as it were,
by measured movements and in a distinct variety of forms.
This eternal Form is neither contained by nor, as it were,
spread out in space, neither prolonged nor changed by time.
Through eternal Form every temporal thing can receive its
form and, in accordance with its kind, can manifest and embody number in space and time.

XVII.
All good things come from God.

A.   Just as we say that something which can be changed   172
is "changeable," so I call that which can receive form "formable," and say that everything that is changeable must also be
formable. Nothing can give itself form, since nothing can give
to itself what it does not have. And surely a thing receives
form so that it may have form. Therefore, if anything what-

ever has a form, it does not need form. But, if something does not have form, it cannot receive from itself what it does not have. Nothing, therefore, as we said, can give itself form.

173   What more should we say concerning the mutability of body and spirit? Enough has been said above. We have established that body and spirit are given form by an immutable and eternal Form. To this Form it has been said, "Thou shalt change them and they will be changed; but thou art the same, and thy years fail not." [1] The speech of the prophet has used "years without fail" to mean "eternity." Concerning this Form, it has been said also that it is "permanent in itself, it renews all things." [2]

174   We understood from this that everything is governed by providence. If all existing things cease to exist when form is completely taken away, immutable Form itself—through which all mutable things subsist, so that they manifest and embody number appropriate to their forms—this immutable Form is their providence, for if it did not exist, they would not exist either.

As he gazes attentively at the whole of creation, he who travels the road to wisdom perceives how delightfully wisdom reveals itself to him on the way, and meets him in all providence. The more beautiful is the road to the wisdom toward which he hastens, the more ardently he burns to complete the journey.

175   If you can find any other kind of creature except [1] that which exists and does not live, or [2] that which lives and does not understand, or [3] that which exists, lives, and understands—only then can you tell me that there exists some good which does not come from God. These three kinds of things can be expressed as well by the two terms, "body" and "life," for what only lives, but does not understand—for example, a beast—and what understands—for example, man—

176   are both properly spoken of as "life." These two, therefore, body and life, which are considered creatures (for one even

1 Ps. 101:27–28 (Ps. 102:26–27).
2 Wisd. of Sol. 7:27.

speaks of the life of the Creator, and this is the highest life)—these two creatures, body and life, since, as we have shown above, they are both formable, and since they dissolve into nothing if form is completely lost, prove that they exist as a result of that Form which is always of the same nature. Therefore, all good things, whether great or small, can come only from God.

What is greater in creatures than life that has understanding? What can be less than body? No matter how much creatures may lack, and however much they tend toward nonexistence by virtue of their deficiency, nevertheless some form remains in them, so that they somehow exist. Moreover, whatever form remains in a deficient object comes from that Form which knows no lack and which does not allow the motions of things, whether they be growing or decaying, to exceed the laws of their own numbers. 177

Therefore, whatever we find to be praiseworthy in nature, whether we judge that its value be great or small, must be referred to the most excellent and ineffable praise of the Creator. Do you have any objections to raise on these points?

XVIII.
Freedom of the will, though it may be abused, is good and divinely given, since without it no one could live rightly.

E. I admit that I am quite convinced—insofar as it can be proved in this life among such as we—that God exists and that all goods are from God, since all things that exist are from God, whether they understand, live, and exist, or whether they live and exist only, or whether they merely exist. Now let us turn to a third question: whether we can establish that free will is to be numbered among the goods. When this has been proven, I will grant without hesitation that God gave us free will, and that He was right to have given it. 178

A. You have remembered well the points we proposed to discuss, and have seen clearly that the second question has 179 already been answered. But you should also have seen that the third question, too, is already solved.

You said you thought that free choice of the will ought not to have been given because through it man sins. To this opinion I replied that no righteous act could be performed except by free choice of the will, and I asserted that God gave it for this reason. You replied that free will ought to have been given as justice was given, so that no one could make evil use 180 of it. This answer of yours forced us to go into a long circuitous course of argument, by which we proved that both greater and lesser goods came only from God. This could not be proved conclusively until we had met the wicked and foolish objections of the fool who "hath said in his heart, 'There is no God.' " [1] Whatever reasoning we performed, within our limited means, concerning such a great question was directed toward what was obvious, with God Himself assisting us in so 181 perilous a course. These two facts, nevertheless, that God exists and that all goods come from Him, were thus discussed—even though we previously believed them in firm faith—in such a way that this third question, that free will is to be numbered among the goods, might also appear in the clearest light.

182   In the previous argument, we proved and established that the nature of the body is on a lower plane than that of the spirit, and because of this, the spirit is a greater good than the body. If, therefore, we find among the goods of the body some that a man can use wrongly, but that we cannot say ought not to have been given to man, since we have agreed that they are goods, why should we wonder if there are in the spirit certain goods, of which we can make wrong use, but which, because they are goods, could not have been given by anyone but Him from whom all good things proceed?

183   Indeed, you see how great a good is wanting to any body that has no hands; yet he who works cruel or shameful deeds with his hands uses them for evil. Should you see someone

1 Ps. 52:1.

without feet, you would acknowledge what an important good was lacking to make his body complete. Yet you would not deny that the man who made evil use of his feet, either for injuring another or for dishonoring himself, was using his feet wrongfully.

With our eyes we see light and distinguish the forms of 184 bodies. The faculty of sight is the fairest in our body, and therefore the eyes are placed, as it were, in the highest position, the place of honor. We use our eyes for keeping safe and for serving life in many other ways. Yet many men commit many shameful deeds by means of their eyes, and force their eyes into the service of lust. You see what a great good the face would lack if there were no eyes; but when we possess them, who gave them but God, the Giver of all good things?

Just as you approve those goods of the body and, disre- 185 garding the people who make evil use of them, you praise Him who gave them, so you should admit that free will, without which no one can live rightly, is good and divinely given; and you should grant that those who make evil use of free will ought to be condemned, rather than saying that He who gave it ought not to have given it.

E. First, however, I wish that you would prove to me 186 that free will is a good. Then I will grant that God gave it to us, since I acknowledge that all goods proceed from God.

A. Did I not prove this to you in the great toils of our 187 earlier discussion, when you agreed that every type and form of body is derived from the Form which is supreme over all things, that is, from Truth, and when you acknowledged also that it is a good? For the Truth itself speaks out in the Gospel that even the hairs of our head are numbered.[2] Have you forgotten what we said about the supremacy of number and its power which extends for ever and ever? What perversity that 188 is! To count the hairs of our head, however scant and useless they may be, among the goods and to find that they can be attributed to no other cause than to God, the Cause of all

2 Matt. 10:30.

goods, since the greatest and the least come from Him; yet to
hesitate on the question of free will, without which even men
who lead the most evil lives agree that they cannot live rightly!

189   Tell me now, please, which you think is better in us: that
without which we can live rightly or that without which we
cannot live rightly?

E.   Please excuse me; I am ashamed of my blindness.
Who would doubt that the more excellent thing by far is that
without which there is no righteous life?

A.   You will not deny then that a blind man can live
rightly?

E.   May I never be so foolish!

A.   Since, then, you admit that the eye in the body is a
good although its loss will not prevent us from living rightly,
will you think that free will is not a good when no one can
live rightly without it?

190   Look at justice, which no one uses wrongly. This is numbered among the highest goods of the mind and among all
the virtues of the soul, upon which an upright and righteous
life depends. No one uses wisdom, courage, or temperance for
evil; for in these as in justice, which you have just mentioned,
right reason [recta ratio] prevails, and without it virtues cannot exist. No one can use right reason for evil.

XIX.
Of the three classes of goods, great, intermediate, and lowest, freedom of the will is an intermediate good.

191   A.   These are great goods. Yet remember that not only
the great goods but also the least ones can be from no one
other than Him from whom all goods proceed, namely from
God. Our previous argument proved that, and you have already gladly given your assent to it.

Therefore the virtues, by which men live rightly, are great
goods, while all kinds of physical beauty [species], without
which men can live rightly, are the lowest goods. The powers

of the spirit, without which no one can live rightly, are the
intermediate goods [*media bona*] between these two. No one   192
uses the virtues for evil. However the other goods, the lowest
and the intermediate ones, can be used not only for good, but
also for evil. No one uses virtues for evil because the very action of a virtue is the good use of those things that we can
also use for evil. Moreover, no one can make wrong use of
using a thing rightly. Therefore, the abundant generosity of
God's goodness is responsible not only for the great goods, but
for the intermediate and lowest goods as well. His goodness
ought to be praised more in the case of the greatest goods
than in that of the intermediate ones, and more in the case
of the intermediate goods than the lowest; but more in all
goods than if He had not bestowed all.

E.   I agree. But the following troubles me, since it in-   193
volves free will, and we see that free will uses some things for
good and some for evil: how is free will to be counted among
those goods which we use?

A.   In the same way as we know by reason everything   194
that we know, and nevertheless even reason itself is numbered
among the things that we know by reason. Have you forgotten that when we asked what is known by reason, you admitted that reason was known by reason? Do not wonder,   195
then, that we can use the free will by means of itself, if we use
other things through our free will. As reason, knowing other
things, also knows itself, so the free will, which makes use of
other things, also makes use of itself. So also memory grasps
not only all the other things which we remember, but also
retains itself in us, because we do not forget that we have a
memory. It remembers not only other things, but also itself;
through memory, in other words, we remember ourselves,
other things, and memory itself.

When the will, which is an intermediate good, clings to   196
immutable good, and this good is not private but is common
to all (like truth, about which we have said much, though
nothing really worthy of it), then man leads a happy life. The
happy life—that disposition of the spirit which clings to im-

mutable goods—is man's proper and primary good. In this
good lie all the virtues that man cannot use for evil. For
although these goods are great and most important in man,
it is known that they belong to each man, and are not common. But it is by clinging to truth and wisdom, which are
common to all, that all men may become wise and happy.

Moreover, one man does not become happy because of another man's happiness. This is because even when he seeks
to be happy by imitating another, he desires to become happy
through that by which he saw the other man made happy,
that is, by immutable truth, which is common to all.

No one becomes prudent through another's prudence, or
brave through another's courage, or temperate through another's temperance. So too, no one becomes just through the
justice of another. Instead, man obtains virtues by adapting
his spirit to the immutable rules and lights of those virtues
which dwell incorruptible in truth itself and in common wisdom, to which the virtuous man has adapted himself and
fitted his spirit. The man seeking virtue has determined to
imitate this spirit, because it is endowed with virtue. Therefore the will, clinging to common and immutable goods, obtains the first and great goods of man, although it is itself
only an intermediate good. The will, however, commits sin
when it turns away from immutable and common goods, toward its private good, either something external to itself or
lower than itself. It turns to its own private good when it desires to be its own master; it turns to external goods when
it busies itself with the private affairs of others or with whatever is none of its concern; it turns to goods lower than itself
when it loves the pleasures of the body. Thus a man becomes
proud, meddlesome, and lustful; he is caught up in another
life which, when compared to the higher one, is death. Yet he
is ruled by the administration of divine providence, which
places everything in its proper order [*ordinat*] and gives to
each what is his own. So it follows that [1] neither the goods
desired by sinners, nor the free will itself which we found to
have been numbered among certain intermediate goods, are

evil in any way, and that [2] evil is a turning away from immutable goods and a turning toward changeable goods. This turning away [*aversio*] and turning toward [*conversio*] result in the just punishment of unhappiness, because they are committed, not under compulsion, but voluntarily.

XX.
The movement of the will from immutable to transient goods, since it is evil, is not from God.

A.   Because the will is moved when it turns from an   201
immutable good to a changeable one, you may perhaps ask
how this movement arises. For the movement itself is certainly evil, although the free will must be numbered among
the goods, because without it no one can live rightly. Even
if this movement, that is, the turning of the will from the
Lord God, is without doubt a sin, we cannot say, can we,
that God is the cause of sin? This movement will not be   202
from God, but what then is its origin? If I should answer
your question by saying that I do not know, you would perhaps be disappointed; yet that would be the truth, for that
which is nothing cannot be known. Only hold to your firm
faith, since no good thing comes to your perception, understanding, or thought which is not from God. Nothing of any   203
kind can be discovered which is not from God. Wherever you
see measure, number, and order, you cannot hesitate to attribute all these to God, their Maker. When you remove measure, number, and order, nothing at all remains. Even if the
beginning of some form were to remain, where you do not find
order or measure or number (since wherever these exist, form
is complete), you must remove even that very beginning of
form which seems to be the artisan's raw material. If the completion of form [*formae perfectio*] is a good, there is some good
even in the rudimentary beginning of form. Thus, if all good   204
is completely removed, no vestige of reality persists; indeed,
nothing remains. Every good is from God. There is nothing

of any kind that is not from God. Therefore, since the movement of turning away from good, which we admit to be sin, is a defective movement [*defectivus motus*] and since, moreover, every defect comes from nothing, see where this movement belongs: you may be sure that it does not belong to God.

Yet since this defect [*defectus*] is voluntary, it lies within our power. You must not be willing to fear this defect, for if you do not desire it, it will not exist. What greater security can there be than to live a life where what you do not will cannot happen to you? Since a man cannot rise of his own will as he fell by his own will, let us hold with firm faith the right hand of God, Jesus Christ our Lord, which is stretched out to us. Let us wait for Him with steadfast hope; let us love Him with burning love.

If, however—though I myself do not think it necessary— you think that we ought to examine the question of the origin of sin more carefully, let us put it off for some other discussion.

E.   I follow your will gladly. Let us postpone to some other time the points suggested in this discussion. I will not, however, grant to you that enough has been said on the subject.

BOOK THREE

I.
How does that movement by which the will is turned from God come about?

Evodius.   Since it is quite clear to me that free will is to be   1
numbered among the goods, and indeed not among the low-
est of these, we are forced to admit that it was a gift of God
and that He acted rightly in giving it. If you think that this
is the right occasion, I would like to know from you the
origin of that movement [*motus*] by which the will is turned
away from common and immutable goods, and toward goods
of its own or those of others, that is, the lowest goods and
every kind of transitory good.

Augustine.   Why do we have to know this?   2

E.   Because if free will has been given in such a way that
this movement is natural to it, then it is turned to lesser goods
by necessity. There is no blame to be found where nature and
necessity rule.

A.   Does this movement please or displease you?

E.   It displeases me.

A.   Then you censure it.

E.   Yes, I do.

A.   You censure, then, a movement of the spirit which
is blameless.

E.   I do not censure a blameless movement of the spirit;
I simply do not know whether there is any blame attached
to leaving an immutable good and turning to those that are
changeable.

A.   You censure, then, what you do not know.

E.   Do not twist my words. I said "I do not know
whether there is any blame" because I wished it to be understood beyond a doubt that there is blame. With the words
"I do not know" I ridiculed doubt about a thing so obvious.

3   *A.*   Let us examine why this truth, which has forced you to forget so soon what you said a moment ago, is so indubitable. If this movement exists naturally and necessarily, it cannot be blameworthy at all. But you believe so firmly that it is blameworthy that you think it ridiculous to doubt a thing so certain. Why, therefore, do you think that a thing which you yourself just proved to be patently false is still
4   to be asserted or spoken of with some doubt? You just said, "If free will has been given in such a way that this movement is natural to it, then it is turned to lesser goods by necessity. There is no blame to be found where nature and necessity rule." You should have known with certainty that the movement does not lie in the nature of the will, since you are so certain that it deserves blame.

5   *E.*   I myself have said that the movement is blameworthy and that it is therefore displeasing to me. I cannot doubt that it is to be blamed. I deny, however, that the soul is to be blamed, when it is dragged by this movement from immutable to transitory goods, if its nature is such that it is moved by necessity.

6   *A.*   To what does this motion, which you grant is surely to be blamed, belong?

E.   I see it in the spirit, but I do not know what it belongs to.

A.   You do not deny, do you, that the spirit is moved by this motion?

E.   Of course not.

A.   Do you deny that the movement by which a stone is moved is the stone's movement? I do not mean the movement by which we move the stone, or when it is moved by some outside force, as when it is thrown into the air; but I mean the movement with which the stone by itself swerves toward the earth and falls.

7   *E.*   Indeed, I admit that the motion you have just described is that of the stone, but it is a natural motion; if the soul also has a movement of this kind, it too is surely natural. It is not right to blame it because of the fact that the move-

ment arose naturally. For even if the movement is toward ruin, it is driven by the necessity of its own nature. However, since we do not deny that the movement is blameworthy, we must deny that it is natural. Therefore, it is not similar to the natural movement by which the stone is moved.

A.   Did we establish anything by our two earlier discussions?   8

E.   Of course!

A.   I believe you remember that in the first discussion we established that the mind could not become a slave of lust except through its own will. It cannot be forced to serve lust by something superior, or by an equal, because this is unjust; also, it cannot be forced by something inferior, because the inferior thing does not have the power. We conclude, therefore, that the movement which, for the sake of pleasure, turns the will from the Creator to the creature belongs to the will itself. If this movement is accounted a defect (and you admit that anyone who doubts this deserves ridicule), then it is not natural, but voluntary. It is in this respect like the movement of the stone which is carried downward, because, as the one movement belongs to the stone, so the other belongs to the spirit. However, it is unlike the movement of the stone in that the stone does not have it in its power to check its downward motion, whereas so long as the spirit does not will to neglect higher goods and love lesser ones, it does not move in that direction. Therefore, the   10 movement of a stone is natural, while that of the spirit is voluntary.   9

This is the reason that, if someone says that a stone sins because it falls downwards through its weight, I will not say he is more senseless than a stone; he is simply insane. But we accuse a spirit of sin when we prove that it has preferred to enjoy lower goods and has abandoned higher ones. Why   11 do we have to inquire into the origin of this movement by which the will is turned from immutable to transitory goods, when we admit that it belongs to the spirit alone, and that it is voluntary and therefore blameworthy? All useful teaching

on this point has its value in the fact that when this movement is disapproved and controlled, we may turn our will
away from the inclination toward temporal things, to the enjoyment of eternal good.

12   *E.*   I understand. I almost touch and grasp the truth of
which you speak. For there is nothing that I feel so deeply
and strongly as that I have a will, through which I move to
enjoy something. I find nothing which I can call my own if
the will by which I accept or reject objects of choice is not
my own will. Therefore, if I do any wrong through it, to
whom but to myself can the wrongdoing be ascribed? Since,
indeed, a good God made me, I cannot do any good except by
my will. It is quite clear that a good God gave me the will
13   for this purpose. If the movement by which the will is turned
this way and that were not voluntary and within our power,
we could not be praised when we turn toward higher things,
or blamed when, as if on a pivot, we turn toward lower ones;
and a man should not be admonished to neglect the temporal
and seek the eternal, or to will to live rightly, not wickedly—
yet he who thinks that we should not be so admonished ought
to be banished from the company of men.

II.
Is God's foreknowledge inconsistent with man's freedom?

14   *E.*   Since this is so, I am deeply troubled by a certain
question: how can it be that God has foreknowledge of all
future events, and yet that we do not sin by necessity? Anyone
who says that an event can happen otherwise than as God has
foreknown it is making an insane and malicious attempt to
15   destroy God's foreknowledge. If God, therefore, foreknew that
a good man would sin (and you must grant this, if you admit
with me that God foreknows all future events)—if this is the
case, I do not say that God should not have made the man,
for He made him good, and the sin of the man He made cannot hurt God at all (on the contrary, in making him, God
showed His goodness, for He showed His justice in punishing

the man and His mercy in forgiving him); I do not say that
God should not have made the man, but I do say this: since
He foreknew that the man would sin, the sin was committed
of necessity, because God foreknew that it would happen.
How can there be free will where there is such inevitable
necessity?

   A.   You have knocked vigorously at the door of God's   16
mercy. May it be opened to those who knock. Yet I do believe that a great number of men are tormented by this question for no other reason than that they do not ask it in the
right way, but are too swift to excuse their sins, instead of
confessing them. For some gladly believe that there is no   17
divine providence in charge of human affairs; abandoning
themselves, their spirits, and their bodies to the accidents of
chance, they give themselves over to be battered and torn by
lusts; they deny divine justice and evade the justice of men.
They try to rid themselves of those who accuse them by appealing to the patronage of Fortune, who is usually portrayed
in statues and pictures as blind; thus, they admit either that
they are better than Fortune, by whom they think they are
ruled, or that they speak and think with the same blindness.
It is not absurd to admit that such men do everything by
chance [*casibus*] when they fall [*cadunt*] because of their actions. But in our second discourse, I think, we sufficiently refuted this opinion, which is so full of stupid and senseless
error. Other men do not dare to deny that the providence of   18
God presides over human life, but still they prefer to believe,
through a wicked error, that the providence of God is weak,
or unjust, or evil, instead of piously and humbly confessing
their sins. If all of these would allow themselves to be per-   19
suaded that, when they think about what is best, most just,
and most powerful, they should believe that the goodness,
justice, and power of God are by far greater than, and superior to, anything they conceive in thought; when they reflect upon themselves, they should understand that they
would be obliged to give thanks to God even if He had willed
them to be lower than they are, and that they should cry out
with the very bone and fiber of their consciousness, "I have

said: Lord have mercy on me, cure my soul, because I have
sinned against you" [1]—then the paths of divine mercy would
lead them into wisdom; through knowledge, they would become better able to see; through ignorance, they would become more humble in their search; yet they would not be
puffed up by success or disheartened by failure in seeking out
20   the truth. I have no doubt that you are already persuaded of
this; but observe how easily I shall answer such an important
question for you after you have given a few answers to my
questions.

III.
God's foreknowledge does not exclude man's freedom in sinning.

21   *A.*   Surely this is the question that troubles and perplexes you: how can the following two propositions, that [1]
God has foreknowledge of all future events, and that [2] we
do not sin by necessity but by free will, be made consistent
with each other? "If God foreknows that man will sin," you
say, "it is necessary that man sin." If man must sin, his sin
is not a result of the will's choice, but is instead a fixed and
22   inevitable necessity. You fear now that this reasoning results
either in the blasphemous denial of God's foreknowledge or,
if we deny this, the admission that we sin by necessity, not
by will. Or does some other point bother you?

E.   No, nothing else right now.

A.   You think that all things of which God has foreknowledge come about by necessity, and not by will?

E.   Absolutely.

23   *A.*   Now pay careful attention. Look at yourself a little
and tell me this, if you can: how are you going to will tomorrow, to sin or to act rightly?

E.   I do not know.

A.   Do you think that God does not know either?

E.   Of course I do not.

A.   If God knows what you are going to will tomorrow

1 Ps. 40:5 (Ps. 41:4).

and foresees how all men who exist now or will exist are going to will in the future, He foresees much more what He will do about just men and about wicked ones.

E.   Yes. If God foreknows my deeds, I would say much more confidently that He foreknows His own deeds and foresees most certainly what He will do.

A.   If everything of which God has foreknowledge hap-   24
pens, not by will, but by necessity, shouldn't you be careful lest you say that God does what He is going to do by necessity too, and not by will?

E.   When I said that everything that God foreknows happens by necessity, I meant only those things which occur in His creation, not what occurs in Himself, since these latter are eternal.

A.   By this reasoning, God is not involved in His own creation.

E.   He has decided once and for all how the order of   25
the universe He created is to be carried out, and does not arrange anything by a new act of will.

A.   Does He not make anyone happy?

E.   Yes, He does.

A.   Then He is responsible when someone becomes happy.

E.   Yes.

A.   If, then, for example, you are to be happy a year from now, He will make you happy a year from now.

E.   Yes.

A.   Therefore, God foreknows today what He will do in a year.

E.   He has always foreknown this. I also agree that He also foreknows it now if it is going to be so.

A.   Please tell me: it is not the case, is it, that you are   26
not His creature? Won't your happiness occur in you?

E.   Of course! I am His creature and my happiness will occur in me.

A.   Therefore, your happiness will come about in you, not by will, but by the necessity of God's action.

E.   God's will is my necessity.

A.   So you will be happy against your will!

E.   Had I the power to be happy, I would surely be
happy now. I wish to be happy now, and am not, because it
is God, not I, who makes me happy.

27   *A.*   How clearly truth cries out from you! For you could
not maintain that anything is in our power except actions
that are subject to our own will. Therefore, nothing is so
completely in our power as the will itself, for it is ready at
hand to act immediately, as soon as we will. Thus we are
right in saying that we grow old by necessity, not by will; or
that we die by necessity, not by will, and so on. Who but a
madman would say that we do not will with the will?

28   Therefore, though God foreknows what we shall will in the
future, this does not prove that we do not will anything voluntarily. In regard to happiness, you said (as if I would deny
it) that you do not make yourself happy. I say, however, that
when you are to be happy, you shall not be happy against
your will, but because you will to be happy. When, therefore,
God foreknows that you will be happy, it cannot be otherwise, or else there would be no such thing as foreknowledge.
Nevertheless, we are not forced to believe, as a consequence
of this, that you are going to be happy when you do not want
29   to be. This is absurd and far from the truth. Moreover, just
as God's foreknowledge, which today is certain of tomorrow's
happiness, does not take from you the will to be happy when
you begin to be happy; in the same way, a will which deserves
blame, if it is going to be blameworthy, will nonetheless remain a will, since God foreknew that it would be so.

30   See, please, how blindly a man says, "If God has foreknown
my will, it is necessary that I will what God foreknows, since
nothing can occur except as he has foreknown it. If, moreover, my act of will is subject to necessity, we must admit that
I willed it not by will, but by necessity." Strange foolishness!
How could it be that nothing happens otherwise than as God
foreknew, if He foreknows that something is going to be willed
31   when nothing is going to be willed? I pass over the equally
astounding assertion that I just said this man makes: "It is

necessary that I will in this way." By assuming necessity, he tries to exclude will. If it is necessary that he will, how can he will, if there is no will?

If he says, in another way, that since it is necessary that he 32 will, this very will is not in his power, he is to be answered with what I just said when I asked whether you would be happy without willing it. You answered that you would be happy if it were in your power to be happy, and that you wanted to, but were not yet able. Then I interposed that the truth had cried out from you because we cannot deny that we have the power, unless we cannot obtain what we will through an act of will or unless the will is absent. When we will, if the will itself is lacking in us, we surely do not will. If it 33 cannot happen that when we will we do not will, then the will is present in the one who wills. And nothing else is in our power except what is present to us when we will. Our will, therefore, is not a will unless it is in our power. And since it is indeed in our power, it is free in us. What we do not, or cannot, have in our power is not free for us. So it 34 follows that we do not deny that God has foreknowledge of all things to be, and yet that we will what we will. For when He has foreknowledge of our will, it is going to be the will that He has foreknown. Therefore, the will is going to be a will because God has foreknowledge of it. Nor can it be a will if it is not in our power. Therefore, God also has knowledge of our power over it. So the power is not taken from me by His fore- 35 knowledge; but because of His foreknowledge, the power to will will more certainly be present in me, since God, whose foreknowledge does not err, has foreknown that I shall have the power.

E.   I no longer deny that whatever God foreknows must come to be, and that he foreknows our sins in such a way that our will still remains free in us and lies in our power.

IV.
God's knowledge that man will sin is not the cause of sin. Hence punishment for sin is just.

36   *A.*   What is it, then, that bothers you? Have you perhaps forgotten what our first argument accomplished? Will
you deny that we sin by will and not under compulsion from
anyone, either higher, lower, or equal?

37   *E.*   Of course I do not dare deny any of these points.
Yet I still cannot see how God's foreknowledge of our sins
can be reconciled with our free choice in sinning. God must,
we admit, be just and have foreknowledge. But I would like
to know by what justice God punishes sins which must be;
or how it is that they do not have to be, when He foreknows
that they will be; or why anything which is necessarily done
in His creation is not to be attributed to the Creator.

38   *A.*   Why do you think that our free choice is opposed
to God's foreknowledge? Is it simply because it *is* foreknowledge or, rather, because it is God's foreknowledge?

      E.   Because it is God's.

      A.   If you foreknew that someone was going to sin,
would it not be necessary for him to sin?

      E.   Yes, he would have to sin, for my foreknowledge
would not be genuine unless I foreknew what was certain.

      A.   Then it is not because it is God's foreknowledge that
what He foreknew had to happen, but only because it is foreknowledge. It is not foreknowledge if it does not foreknow
what is certain.

      E.   I agree. But why are you making these points?

39   *A.*   Because unless I am mistaken, your foreknowledge
that a man will sin does not of itself necessitate the sin. Your
foreknowledge did not force him to sin even though he was,
without doubt, going to sin; otherwise you would not foreknow that which was to be. Thus, these two things are not
contradictories. As you, by your foreknowledge, know what
someone else is going to do of his own will, so God forces no

one to sin; yet He foreknows those who will sin by their own will.

Why cannot He justly punish what He does not force to be   40
done, even though He foreknows it? Your recollection of
events in the past does not compel them to occur. In the same
way God's foreknowledge of future events does not compel
them to take place. As you remember certain things that you
have done and yet have not done all the things that you remember, so God foreknows all the things of which He Himself is the Cause, and yet He is not the Cause of all that He
foreknows. He is not the evil cause of these acts, though He
justly avenges them. You may understand from this, therefore, how justly God punishes sins; for He does not do the
things which He knows will happen. Besides, if He ought not   41
to exact punishment from sinners because He foresees that they
will sin, He ought not to reward those who act rightly, since in
the same way He foresees that they will act rightly. On the contrary, let us acknowledge both that it is proper to His foreknowledge that nothing should escape His notice and that it
is proper to His justice that a sin, since it is committed voluntarily, should not go unpunished by His judgment, just as it
was not forced to be committed by His foreknowledge.

V.
God is to be praised, not blamed, even for His creation of beings who are able to sin and subject to unhappiness.

A.   Now for the point that you put third in order: can   42
we avoid attributing to the Creator anything that happens of
necessity in His creation? In considering this question, we
should recall that rule of piety which will readily admonish
us that we owe thanks to our Creator, whose generous goodness should most justly be praised even if He had made us
creatures of some lower order. For although our soul is wasted   43
by sins, still it is loftier and better than it would be if it were
turned into the light seen by our eyes. Surely you see how

much praise even those souls that have surrendered to the senses of the body give to God for the excellence of light. Therefore, do not be bothered by the fact that sinful souls are blamed, so that you say in your heart, "It would have been better if they had never existed." They are blamed in comparison with themselves, because one reflects upon what they might have been if they had not willed to sin. Yet God their Maker should be given the highest praise that men can give, not only because He places sinners in a just order [*juste ordinat*], but also because He made sinners in such a way that, even when soiled with sin, they still surpass the excellence of corporeal light which is, however, quite justly praised.

45   I warn you also to beware of this: you should avoid saying not only, "It would have been better if they had not existed," but also, "They ought to have been made differently." If, by true reasoning, you conceive of something better, you can be sure that God, the Creator of all good, has already made it. Moreover, it is not true reasoning, but simply an envious weakness, if you wish that the lower should not have been made because you think that something higher should have been created. It is as if, because you had looked upon the heavens, you wished that there be no earth. That would be totally wrong. You would then quite justly find fault if you should see the earth created, but the heavens not. You might then say that the earth should have been made like your conception of the heavens. You ought to feel no envy at all when you see that the very thing has already been created after whose likeness you wanted to pattern the earth and that it is called, not earth, but the heavens; for I think you would not be deprived of a better thing so that something lower, namely the earth, might come into being. Moreover, so great is the variety of earthly things that we can conceive of nothing which belongs to the form of the earth in its full extent which God, the Creator of all things, has not already created. For you may proceed by degrees through intermediate types of land, from the most fruitful and delightful to the most

treacherous and sterile, so that you would not dare to find any
fault except in comparison with what is better. Thus you
would ascend through all degrees of praise until you found
the highest type of land—which, nonetheless, you would not
want to be the only type in existence. How great is the dis- 48
tance between the whole earth and the sky? There lies between them a watery nature and an airy one. From these four
elements we derive a variety of forms and species which God
has numbered, although we cannot count them. There can 49
exist in nature things which your reason is incapable of con-
ceiving. It cannot be, however, that what you conceive with
true reason cannot exist. You cannot conceive of anything
better in creation which has escaped the Maker of the creation. The human soul is naturally connected with divine
ideas [divinae rationes], upon which it depends when it says,
"This would be better than that." If the soul speaks with
truth and understanding, it does so because of those divine
ideas with which it is connected. The soul should believe that 50
God made that which it knows, by true reason, ought to have
been made by Him, even if it does not see this in actuality.
Even if a man could not see the heavens with his eyes, still
he could grasp, by true reason, that some such thing ought to
have been created. The soul ought to believe that the heavens
were made, even if it were unable to see them with its own
eyes. For the soul would not have understood through
thought that the heavens ought to have been made, if this
conception were not among those ideas through which all
things were made. What does not participate in the divine
ideas cannot be grasped by true understanding, since it is
itself not true.

Many men make mistakes on this point, for when they 51
conceive of better things with their minds, they seek them
with their eyes in inappropriate places. It is just as if a man,
who grasped by his reason perfect roundness, became dis-
gusted because he could never discover roundness in a nut—
never having seen any other round body except fruit of this
sort. The superiority of a creature who, though he possesses a 52

free will, is never guilty of sin because of his dedication to God, is perfectly obvious to men. But when they observe human sin, they complain about the fact that man was created, instead of the fact that he is guilty of sin. Hence they say, "God should have made us so that we might enjoy His im-

53 mutable truth, and never will to sin." They ought not to cry out or be angry. Because God made men and gave them the power to choose what they want, He did not force them to sin. There are some angels who are such that they have never sinned and who never will. If you delight in the creature who avoids sin with a most persistent will, you would doubtless prefer him

54 to the sinner in accordance with right reason. Just as you estimate him more highly in your reasoning, so God the Creator ranks him more highly in the ordering of His creation. You should then believe that there is a sinless creature in higher places and in the heights of the heavens; because if our Creator showed His goodness in creating a creature whose future sins He foresaw, He would by all means show His goodness in

55 creating a creature who He foreknew would not sin. Such a sublime creature has perpetual happiness and enjoys his Creator forever. He merits this because of his unalterable will to hold to justice. The sinful creature also has his own place in God's order, and although he has lost his happiness through sin, he has not lost the power to recover this happiness. He is surely better than the creature who forever wills to sin, and he is a kind of mean [*medietas*] between this latter creature and the sinless creature we mentioned before, who forever has his will fixed on justice. This creatures reaches his

56 highest place through the humility of repentance. God did not withhold the abundance of His goodness from the creature who He foreknew would both sin and continue to sin willfully, by refusing to create him. Just as a stray horse is better than a stone which is not astray, since the stone does not have its own motion or perception, so the creature who sins with his free will is more excellent than the creature who

57 does not sin because he has no free will. I would praise, as

well, wine which is good in itself, and yet I would censure a man who got drunk on that very wine. I would still prefer the drunken man whom I just censured to the wine I praised, which made the man drunk. Thus, the corporeal creature is rightly to be praised on its own level [*in suo gradu*], while those who are kept by immoderate drinking from the perception of truth are to be censured. The very men who have been corrupted and are reeling because of that same creature which on its level is praiseworthy and through greed for which men have been ruined—these very men have a higher place than that wine, because of the dignity of their nature, not because of their vices. Since, therefore, every soul is better 58 than any body whatsoever; since every sinful soul, however far it may have fallen, cannot be changed into a body at all, and the fact that it is a soul cannot be changed—since this is so, it cannot obscure the fact that it is better than a body. Among bodies, moreover, light holds first place. Consequently, the last soul is placed ahead of the first body, and it can happen that the body of one soul may be ranked before the body of another soul, but never can it be ranked before the soul itself.

Therefore God is to be praised with ineffable praise. For 59 when He made the souls which would abide by the laws of justice, He also made other souls, which He foresaw would either sin or continue in sin; yet these souls are still better than those that cannot sin because they have no rational free choice of the will, and these latter souls, in turn, are better than any body whatsoever, however brilliant its radiance. Some men [1] even worship this radiance as the very substance of supreme Godhead, though they do so in great error. But 60 if, in the order of corporeal creatures, the beauty of good things is built by degrees from the very choirs of stars to the hairs of our head, how unreasonably do men say, "What is this? How is this?" For all things have been created in their proper order. How much more unreasonable to say this about

[1] The Manichees.

a soul, which will always without a doubt surpass the dignity
of all bodies, however much it may be degraded and deprived
of beauty.

61   Reason makes its judgments in one way, and common
sense in another. Reason judges by the light of truth so that,
by right judgment, it subordinates lesser things to the more
important ones. Common sense, on the other hand, inclines
toward the habit of convenience, so that it puts a higher value
on those things that truth proves to be of lesser value. While
reason places celestial bodies far over terrestrial ones, what
carnal man would not prefer that the stars be missing from
the sky, rather than a single bush from his field, or a cow
62 from his herd? Men of mature years despise (or else tolerate
until corrected) the judgment of the child who would prefer
the death of a man (except for loved ones) to the death of
his bird—especially if the man is one who frightens him and
the bird a good singer and pretty! So men who have progressed
toward wisdom by maturity of mind usually endure inexperienced judges calmly, when they discover them praising
God for His lesser creatures, which they find better suited to
their carnal senses, instead of praising God in higher and
better things; or praising God too little, trying sometimes to
blame God or improve upon Him, or not believing that God
is the Creator of these things. The judgments of such men
are despised by the mature if they cannot correct them, or
else simply endured with equanimity until they can correct
them.

VI.
No one prefers his own nonexistence
to unhappiness.

63   *A.*   Since this is so, the idea that the sins of a creature
can be attributed to the Creator is far from the truth, even
though things must happen as God foreknows them. While
you say that you cannot see why anything that must happen
in God's creation is not to be attributed to God, I, on the con-

trary, do not and cannot find a way to attribute them to God. Indeed, I would assert that there is no way to impute to God anything that must occur in His creation as a result of the will of sinners.

If a man should say, "I would prefer not to exist than to 64 be unhappy," I would answer, "You lie! For you are unhappy and you do not want to die; proof of this is that you are alive. Even while you do not wish to be unhappy, you have the will to live. Give thanks then that you have the will to live, so that you can cease to be what you do not will to be. For you do will to live, but you do not will to be wretched. If you are ungrateful that you are alive—and you do will to be alive—then you are quite properly constrained to live the kind of life you do not will [i.e., a life of wretchedness]. I praise the goodness of the Creator because you have what you want, even though you are ungrateful for it. I praise the justice of God, the Giver of order [*ordinator*], because you suffer what you do not wish to suffer, [as the penalty] for your ungratefulness."

He may say, "It is not because I would rather be unhappy 65 than not exist at all that I am unwilling to die, but because I fear that after death I may be more unhappy." I shall answer, "If it is unjust for you to be more unhappy after death, you will not be more unhappy. If, however, it is just, let us praise God by whose laws you will be unhappy." Then he may say, "How may I assume that if it is unjust, I shall not be unhappy?" I shall answer, "Because, if you have power over yourself, either you will not be unhappy or, because you rule yourself unjustly, you will be justly unhappy. If you 66 wish to rule yourself justly, yet do not have the power, you will not be in your own power, and will either be in no one's power or in another's. If you are in no one's power, either you do not will to be unhappy or you do so will. But you cannot be anything if you do not will anything, unless some force overpowers you. Furthermore, a man who is not in any-one's power cannot be overpowered by any force. Moreover, if you are not willing to be in anyone's power, reason shows

that you are in your own power. Thus you are justly unhappy, if you rule yourself unjustly; and since you will be
whatever you will, you have reason for giving thanks to the
67   goodness of your Creator. If you are not going to be in your
own power, then surely someone stronger or someone weaker
will hold you in his power. If someone weaker holds you in
his power, it is your fault and your unhappiness is just; for
you could, if you would, overpower a weaker person. If, however, a stronger person holds you in his power, you will not
rightly think such a right ranking in the created order [*ordinatio*] is unjust. Thus I was right when I said, 'If it is unjust
for you to be more unhappy after death, you will not be more
unhappy. If, however, it is just, let us praise God by whose
laws you will be unhappy.' "

VII.
Men love existence, in spite of their unhappiness, because they are from Him who *is* in the highest degree.

68   *A.*   Suppose he should say: "Because I already exist, I
prefer to be unhappy rather than not to exist at all. But if I
could have been consulted before I existed, I would have
chosen not to exist rather than to be unhappy. Now, the fact
that I am afraid not to exist, even though I am unhappy, is
a matter of the unhappiness itself: because of the unhappiness, I do not want what I ought to want, for I ought to will
69   not to exist rather than to be unhappy. As it is, I confess that
I would rather be unhappy than be nothing at all. The more
unhappy I am, the more unwisely I want this; the more I
see that I ought not to want this, the more unhappy I am!"

I shall answer as follows: "Be careful that you do not make
a mistake in the very place where you think that you see the
truth. If you were happy, you would rather be alive than
dead. Now, although you are unhappy, you would rather be
alive (though unhappy) than not exist at all, even though
70   you do not want to be unhappy. Therefore, consider as best

you can what a great good is existence itself [*ipsum esse*], inasmuch as both the unhappy and the happy want it. If you
consider this thoroughly, you will realize that the degree of
your unhappiness is commensurate with your distance from
that which *is* in the highest degree [*quod summe est*]. You
will realize, moreover, that the more you think that it is
better for a man not to be at all than to be unhappy, the
farther you are from seeing that which *is* in the highest degree. Nevertheless, you wish to be because you are from Him
who *is* in the highest degree. Therefore, if you want to avoid   71
unhappiness, love the will to exist which is in you. If, more
and more, you desire to be, you will approach that which *is*
in the highest degree. Give thanks, now, that you *are;* for
although you are inferior to those who are happy, yet you are
superior to the things which do not have the will to be happy
but which, even so, are praised by unhappy men. Nevertheless, all things are to be praised for the very fact that they
exist; for by the very fact that they *are,* they are good. The   72
more you love existence, the more you will desire eternal life.
You will desire to be trained so that your desires may not be
temporal (unjust, that is, and weighed down by the love of
temporal things). As for temporal things, they have no existence before they exist; while they exist, they are passing away;
once they have passed away, they will never exist again. And
so, when temporal things are yet to come, they do not exist;
further, when they are past, they do not exist. How can they   73
be thought to be permanent, when, for them, beginning to
exist is the same as proceeding toward nonexistence? The
man who loves existence approves temporal things insofar as
they exist; but that which exists forever, he loves. If ever he
turns to the love of the temporal, he will be protected by the
love of the eternal. If he wastes himself in the love of the
transient, he will be made firm in the love of the permanent.
He will be constant and gain the very being which he desired
when he was afraid not to be, yet could not be firm because
he was enmeshed in the love of the temporal. Do not, there-   74
fore, despair, but rather rejoice, that you would rather exist,

even unhappy, than not be unhappy because you do not exist. If you add gradually to this beginning, that is, to your will to exist, little by little you will rise and build toward that which *is* in the highest degree. You will be kept from any fall by which the lowest form of existence passes into non-existence and drags down with it the strength of the man who 75   loves it. Hence the man who prefers not to exist so as to avoid unhappiness becomes unhappy because he cannot *not exist.* On the other hand, the man who loves to exist more than he hates to be unhappy may shut out what he hates by adding what he loves. And when he begins to exist perfectly in his own class [*in suo genere*], he will not be unhappy."

VIII.
No one, not even the suicide, freely chooses not to exist.

76   *A.*   See how foolish and inconsistent it is to say, "I would prefer not to be, than to be unhappy." The man who says, "I prefer this to that," chooses something; but "not to be" is not something, but nothing. Therefore, you cannot in any way choose rightly when you choose something that does not exist. You say that you wish to exist although you are un-happy, but that you ought not to wish this. What, then, ought you to have willed? You answer, "Not to exist." But if you ought to have willed not to exist, then "not to exist" is better. 77   However, what does not exist cannot be better; therefore, you should not have willed this. The feeling through which you do not will not to exist is truer than the opinion by which you think that you ought to will not to exist.

Furthermore, a man necessarily becomes better when he achieves what he rightly chose to seek. He who does not exist, however, cannot be better. No one, therefore, can rightly 78   choose not to exist. We should not be impressed by the judg-ment of the men who, in their unhappiness, committed sui-cide. They escaped to where they thought they would be better. But whatever they thought, this is no refutation of our reasoning. If they believed that they would not exist at all, the fallacious choice of men who choose nothing at all is even less disturbing. How can I follow a man who, when I ask him what he chooses, answers that he chooses nothing? The man who chooses not to be, surely chooses to be nothing. Even if he will not give this answer, he is refuted.

Let me summarize, if I can, what I think of this matter: I 79 think that when a man takes his life or somehow wishes to die, he does not have the feeling that he will have life after death, although he may have this opinion. Opinion, whether maintained by reason or by faith, is either true or false, while a feeling prevails either by custom or by nature. That one 80 thing can appeal to opinion and another to feeling is readily seen from the fact that we believe that we ought to do one thing, but we delight in doing another. Sometimes the feeling is closer to the truth than opinion, especially if the feeling is natural and the opinion false, as in the case of a sick man who often wants cold water which would do him good, but nevertheless believes that it will be harmful if he drinks it. Sometimes opinion is closer to the truth than feeling, as in 81 the case of the man who believes the word of doctors that cold water is harmful and nevertheless chooses to drink it in spite of the fact that it is harmful. Sometimes both are true. This occurs when a man not only believes but also desires what is beneficial to him. Sometimes both are wrong, as when what is harmful is believed to be beneficial and does not cease to be desirable.

It is often the case, however, that a right opinion corrects 82 a wrong habit, or that a wrong opinion ruins what is right by nature. So strong is the force of opinion in the dominion and realm of reason! When someone who believes that at his death he will cease to exist is driven by unendurable troubles to yearn for death, he makes his decision and takes his life. He has the false opinion that he will be totally annihilated, but his natural feeling is a longing for peace. What is at 83 peace, however, is not nothing; on the contrary, it exists to a greater degree than something that is not at peace. Restlessness changes a man's emotions so that one feeling destroys another. Peace, however, is constant, and because of this constancy it is said of peace that it exists. Every willful desire for

84   death is directed toward peace, not toward nonexistence. Although a man erroneously believes that he will not exist after death, nevertheless by nature, he desires to be at peace; that is, he desires to *be* in a higher degree. Therefore, just as no one can will in any way not to exist, so no one who exists should be ungrateful for the goodness of the Creator.

IX.
The suffering of sinners is part of the perfection of the created order.

85   *A.*   If he says, "It would not have been difficult or troublesome for an omnipotent God to have created everything so that each would have its own place in the order of creation, in such a way that no one would be wretched; for it is impossible that omnipotence lack power, or that goodness be spiteful," my answer is as follows: the order of creation from the highest to .the lowest occurs by just degrees. The man who speaks in such a way is simply envious when he says that

86   this should have been different, or that that should not be. If he wishes something to be like something else which is higher, the very thing that he wishes to change is so great that it ought not to be changed because it is perfect. For the man who says, "It should have been this way," wishes to add to a higher creation that is already complete. Thus he is unjust and immoderate, for he wishes to destroy this thing; he is

87   evil and spiteful as well. The man who says, "This should not be," is also evil and spiteful, since he does not wish a creature to exist which he is forced to praise even though it is inferior. For example, if a man should say, "The moon should not exist," and yet acknowledge—or foolishly and contentiously deny—that even the light of a lamp is by far inferior, though it has a beauty of its own and is suited to the darkness of the earth and adapted for use at night, and in all

these ways is praiseworthy in its own small way, how could 88
he dare assert that there should be no moon, but that the
moon ought to be like the sun which he sees? He does not
realize that he is simply saying that there should be two
suns, not that there should be no moon. He errs in two ways:
he wishes to add something to perfection when he desires
another sun, and he wishes to diminish perfection when he
wants to do away with the moon.

Perhaps he may say that he does not find fault with the 89
moon's inferior brightness since this inferior brightness does
not make the moon unhappy, but that he does grieve over
souls, not because of their inferior brightness, but because
of their unhappiness. Let him think carefully over the fact
that the moon's brightness is not unhappy and the sun's
radiance is not happy. Although they are celestial bodies, 90
nevertheless they are bodies, so far as concerns the light which
can be discerned by the eyes of the body. For no bodies considered as bodies can be happy or unhappy, although they
may be the bodies of happy or unhappy men. Yet the analogy 91
of the soul with light shows this: in contemplating the difference in bodies, you would be wrong, when you see some
brighter light, in seeking to remove the duller one to make
the lights equal in brightness. By referring everything to the
perfection of the universe, you see that their existence is dependent upon their being brighter or duller. You do not have
a perfect universe except where the presence of greater things
results in the presence of lesser ones, which are needed for
comparison.

You should think about the difference in souls, in which
you will find the unhappiness that grieves you, and you will
recognize that they have the power to complete the perfection of the universe even though, since they will to sin, they
must be unhappy. It is far from the truth to think that God
ought not to have made such souls, even as He made other
creatures who are by far lower than unhappy souls.

That objection is even less reasonable which says that if 92
our unhappiness completes the perfection of the universe, then

there would be imperfection in the universe if we were all happy; for then if the soul can come to happiness only by sinning, even our sins are necessary to the perfection of the universe that God created, and how would God be just in punishing sins? For if there were no sins, His creation would not be full and perfect.

93   In answer to this I say that neither sin nor unhappiness is necessary to the perfection of the universe; rather, it is the souls which, simply because they are souls, are necessary to its perfection. If souls will to sin, they sin. If they have sinned, they become unhappy. If unhappiness were to go on existing even after these souls had ceased to sin, or if happiness preceded sin, the order and government of the universe could properly be said to be ill-formed. If sin occurred and unhappiness did not result from it, then evil would violate order.

94   As long as men who do not sin gain happiness, the universe is perfect. When sinners are unhappy, the universe is perfect. Since there are souls that gain happiness because they do right or unhappiness because they sin, the universe is always full and perfect with respect to each of its natures. Sin and the punishment of sin are not properly natures, but they are conditions of natures. Sin is voluntary and punishment is

95   penal, but the willfully acquired condition which arises from sin is disgraceful. Punishment is used in such a way that it places natures in their right order (that is, where it is not a disgrace for them to be) and forces them to comply with the beauty of the universe, so that the punishment of sin corrects

96   the disgrace of sin. The superior creature who sins may be punished by inferior creatures, since the latter are so base that they can be adorned even by souls in disgrace and so conform to the beauty of the universe. In a house, what is so great as a man, and what so low and base as the house's sewer? Yet the slave caught in some offense, for which he has to clean

97   the sewer, adorns the sewer even by his disgrace; both of these—the slave's disgrace and the cleaning of the sewer—are joined and reduced to a kind of unity. They are fitted and

woven into the household order in such a way that, with their beauty, they suit its world, with its own perfectly ordered beauty. Yet if the slave had not willed to sin, other provisions for cleaning the household necessities would have been made in managing the house. What is so low in nature as the earthly body? Yet a sinful soul so adorns this corruptible flesh 98 that it adds becoming beauty and living motion to the body. Such a soul is not fit, because of sin, for a celestial home, but is fitted for an earthly home through punishment. Whatever the soul chooses, the universe whose Creator and Ruler is God is always beautiful, because it possesses the most appropriate structure possible. When the best souls dwell in the 99 lowest creation, they do not beautify it with unhappiness, which it does not feel, but they beautify it by good use of it. If, however, sinful souls were allowed to dwell in high places, it would be disgraceful, since they do not harmonize with things that they cannot use properly, nor do they add any beauty to them.

Although the terrestrial sphere is numbered among cor- 100 ruptible things, it keeps as best it can the image of higher things and continually shows them to us as examples and signs. If we see a good and a great man burned by fire in the performance of his duty, we call this, not the punishment of sin, but a proof of his courage and endurance. Even though a horrible corruption consumes his corporeal body, we love him even more than if he had not suffered this, and we marvel because the nature of the spirit was not changed by the change in the body. When we see the body of a ruthless criminal con- 101 sumed by a like punishment, we approve the order of the law. Both of these torments, therefore, adorn the world, the first through virtue, the second through sin. If after these fires, or even before them, we should see the noble man changed so as to be fit for a heavenly dwelling and then raised to the stars, we would rejoice. But if we should see the depraved criminal, either before or after punishment, raised to a seat of honor in heaven even though he is still as evil

102 as ever, who would not be indignant? Both men, therefore, adorn the baser creation, but only the good man adorns the higher.

We should note that the first man adorned the mortality of flesh so that the punishment might fit the crime, and that our Lord then adorned the mortality of flesh so that He might free us by His mercy. Unlike the just man—who, abiding in justice, was able to have a mortal body—the wicked man, as long as he is wicked, cannot reach the immortality of saints, that is, sublime and angelic immortality; not the immortality of those angels whom the Apostle said, "Know you not that we shall judge angels?" [1] but those of whom our Lord said, "For they will be equal to the angels of God." [2]

103 Men who, because of their vain glory, want to be equal to the angels, do not really want to be equal to the angels; rather, they want the angels to be equal to them. If they persevere in this wish, they will be equal in punishment to the fallen angels who loved their own power rather than the power of God. When they are placed on the left, because they have not sought God through the door of humility which our Lord Jesus Christ shows in Himself, and because they lived in pride and hardness of heart, to these it will be said, "Depart into eternal fire which has been prepared for the devil and his angels." [3]

X.
What is the role of the devil, and how has God freed man from him?

104 *A.*   Although there are two sources of sin, one from man's unprompted thinking and the other by persuasion from outside, both indeed are voluntary. The prophet refers to this when he writes, "Cleanse me of secret sins and from the sins

[1] I Cor. 6:3.
[2] Luke 20:36.
[3] Matt. 25:41.

of others spare your servant." [1] Both are voluntary because
the one sins through his own thinking while the other yields,
of his own will, to evil persuasion from outside. Nevertheless,
it is more serious to sin of one's own accord without outside
persuasion and to persuade another, through envy and wiles,
to sin, than to be led by another to sin. Therefore, the justice   105
of God is preserved in punishing each of these sins. This also
was weighed in the scales of equity so that man was not
denied the power of the devil himself, who has made man
subject to him through persuasion. It would have been unfair
if man were not in the power of the one who caught him. It is
impossible for the perfect justice of the highest and true God,
which extends to everything, to abandon the just downfall of
sinners. Yet because man has sinned less than the devil, man   106
has the power to regain his salvation for this reason: he was
in bondage, even in the mortality of his flesh, to the prince of
this world, the father of mortal and base things (that is, of all
sins), and the ruler of death. And so, because of his con-   107
sciousness of mortality, man is afraid, and dreads harm and
destruction from the lowest, basest, and tiniest of beasts. He
is uncertain about the future, and unable to control unlawful
pleasure—especially pride, by which man fell. He comes to ruin
by this one vice, pride, through which the remedy of mercy is
rejected. Who is more in need of mercy than an unhappy man?
Who is more unworthy of mercy than a proud and unhappy
man?

From this it has come about that the Word of God,   108
"through which all things were made," [2] and of which all
angelic natures partake, extended His mercy toward our unhappiness, and "the Word was made Flesh and dwelt among us." [3]
Thus man, who was not yet equal to angels, was able to eat
the Bread of angels, if the Bread of angels deigned to become
equal to men. The Word of God did not desert the angels   109

1 Ps. 18:13–14 (Ps. 19:12–13).
2 John 1:3.
3 John 1:14.

when He came to us, but was at the same time wholly theirs and wholly ours. He feeds the angels inwardly by His Godhead, and He admonishes us outwardly by having become flesh. Through faith, He makes us fit to feed like the angels, and He feeds us by appearing to us.

For the rational creature is fed by the Word, which is, as it were, the best Food. The human soul, moreover, is rational, though it is bound by the mortal chains of the punishment of sin. Its rationality is reduced, however, to the point that it must struggle by conjecture about visible things toward an understanding of invisible ones. The Food of the rational creature was made visible not through a change in Its own nature, but by Its being attired in the clothing of our nature, so that It recalls us to invisible things even as we pursue visible ones. In this way, the souls finds Him whom it forsook in pride, outwardly humble, and will imitate His visible humility and return to His invisible height.

110   The Word of God, the only Son of God, made the devil subject even to man, for He has always kept and will always keep him under His laws. He did not take mastery from the devil by violence, but overcame him by the law of justice. After the devil deceived woman and overthrew man by her, he claimed by the law of death all the descendants of the first man, as though they were sinners. He punished them through a malicious desire to do harm, but nonetheless he punishes them most justly. His power lasted until he killed even the Just One in whom he could find nothing worthy of death, because He was killed for no offense at all, and because He was born without lust, to which the devil has subjugated all whom he catches, so as to keep whatever fruit might be born of lust; the devil's desire to keep this fruit was indeed 111   wicked, but his claim to possess them not unfair. He is justly forced to release those who believe in Him whom the devil unjustly killed. And when they die in body, they cancel the debt and live eternally in Him who paid for them what He did not owe. The men whom the devil has persuaded to persist in unbelief are justly kept with the devil in eternal

damnation. Thus it came about that the devil did not take   112
man by force, but caught him by persuasion. And man who
was justly humbled, so that he might serve the devil for whom
he consented to do evil, was justly set free by Him for whom
he consented to do good. This is possible because man sinned
less in giving consent than the devil did in wickedly persuad-
ing him to do evil.

XI.
Men, whether they choose the good or the evil, have a part in the created order.

A.   God made all natures, not only those which will con-   113
tinue in virtue and justice, but also those which will sin. He
did not make them so that they might sin, but so that they
might adorn the universe whether they will to sin or whether
they do not so will. If the universe did not have souls which
could attain the very peak of the order in the whole creation
—such that, if they chose to sin, the universe would be
weakened and would totter something great would be missing in creation; indeed, the universe would lack a thing so
important that once it was removed, the stability and harmony of the creation would be disturbed. The most holy,   114
best, and sublime creatures of heavenly powers, and of the
powers that are above heaven, are like this. God alone commands them. The whole world is subject to them. The universe could not exist without the just and perfect function of
these creatures. Likewise, if the creature did not exist who
could either sin or not sin, the order of the whole universe
would not be diminished, although it would lack something
important. There are, then, souls which are rational and
quite unequal to those angelic creatures in function; but they
are equal in their nature, and there are still many grades of
things created by the highest God which, though inferior to
rational souls, are yet praiseworthy.
        The nature of the sublimer function is this: if it did not   115
exist or even if it should sin, it would detract from the order

of the universe. The nature of the inferior function is such that only if it did not exist (not if it sinned) would the universe be diminished. To the former has been given the power of maintaining all things as its function. This could not be

116   missing from the order of the universe. It does not continue to will the good because it has taken on this function; instead it has this function because God who gave it foreknew that it would continue thus. It does not, however, maintain everything by its own majesty, but by clinging to the majesty, and obeying the commands, of Him "by Whom and through Whom all things were made." [1] To the latter, provided it did not sin, was granted the power of maintaining everything— not as its own, however, but in company with the former creatures of angelic nature inasmuch as it would sin, as was

117   foreknown. These two natures have certain spiritual bonds between them, and they join and separate without adding to, or detracting from, each other. Thus the former angelic nature is not aided in the case of its action when the other is joined to it, nor was its action made more difficult when the other forsook its duty and sinned. Creatures of the spirit can be joined and separated by the likeness or disparity of their natures, but not by place or size, although they may each

118   possess their own bodies. The soul, after it sins, is placed in a lower, mortal body, and does not rule its own body entirely by choice, but only as much as the laws of the universe allow. Yet such a soul is not inferior to a celestial body, although the earthly body is inferior to the celestial one. The rags of a condemned slave are indeed inferior to the clothing of a well-deserving slave who is in his master's good graces. But the slave himself is better than the most costly raiment, because he is a man.

119   The angelic nature, therefore, clings to God in a celestial body with angelic powers, and it adorns and rules an earthly body, just as God, whose will is ineffable, orders. The other nature which is weighed down by a mortal body hardly governs from within the body by which it is oppressed, and yet it

1 John 1:3.

adorns the body as far as possible. It acts as best it can upon
other bodies lying outside of it; but its effect is very feeble.

XII.
The created order would be preserved even if every
angelic creature revolted against God.

A. From the foregoing we know that the least of corpo- 120
real creatures would not have lacked suitable adornment even
if the other nature, that which sins, had been unwilling to
do so; for what can rule the whole can also rule a part of the
whole. But what rules a lesser object cannot necessarily rule
greater things: a perfect doctor can effectively cure the mange,
but it is not necessarily true that the man who can cure the
mange can cure every human disease. Indeed, if we discern 121
the true reason by which it becomes obvious that there must
exist a creature who will never sin, the same reason leads us
to the conclusion that this creature is not forced not to sin,
but abstains from sin of its own free will. Nevertheless, if this 122
creature sinned (although it has never sinned, just as God
foreknew)—if, however, it did sin, the unutterable force of
God's power would suffice to rule the universe in such a way
that, by giving to each what is right and fitting, He would
permit nothing disgraceful or unbecoming in His entire
empire. If God ruled by none of the powers created for rul- 123
ing, and if every angelic creature rebelled in sin against His
teachings, still by His very majesty, God would rule everything in the best and most becoming way. God felt no envy
toward the spiritual creature and its existence; He even has
made corporeal objects far inferior to the spiritual creatures
who sin. Yet He did so with such bountiful goodness that no
one looking rationally upon the sky, the earth, and all the
visible natures—each governed, formed, and set in its proper
place—would believe that there existed any Creator of the
universe other than God, or would they fail to confess that
He should be praised ineffably. Yet even though there is no
order of the universe [*rerum ordinatio*] better than that in

which angelic power, through the perfection of its nature and goodness of its will, is pre-eminent in governing the universe, still, even if all the angels were to sin, the Creator of angels would continue to rule His empire with no defect. This follows because God's goodness knows no disgust nor

124 His omnipotence any difficulty, and He would not fail to create others who could take the places left empty by those who sinned. No matter how many spiritual creatures were deservedly condemned, they could not debase the order which fittingly and properly excludes them. Wherever we direct our thoughts, we discover that God must be praised ineffably as the best Creator of all natures, and as the most just Ruler.

125 Let us leave the contemplation of the beauty of the universe to those who, through a gift of God, can see it, and stop trying to lead men who are unable to contemplate what cannot be expressed; but let us, nevertheless, solve this greater question in the briefest possible argument, for the sake of men who are either loquacious, weak, or cunning.

XIII.
To blame the fault of a creature is to praise its essential nature.

126   *A.*   Every nature which can become less good is good, and every nature becomes less good when it is corrupted. Now, either corruption does not harm the nature and it is not corrupted, or if the nature is corrupted, corruption causes harm; and corruption, if it causes harm, takes something away from the good of the nature and makes the nature less good. Now, if corruption completely removes all good from the nature, what remains cannot be corrupted since there will not exist any good to be removed and harmed by corruption.

127 Moreover, what corruption cannot harm is not corrupted, and the nature which is not corrupted is incorruptible. This line of reasoning leads to the absurd conclusion that a nature will be incorruptible after corruption has occurred. Therefore, the

truth is that every nature, insofar as it is a nature, is good; since if it is incorruptible, it is better than a corruptible nature, and if it is corruptible, it is without doubt good because when it is corrupted, it becomes less good. Every nature, moreover, is either corruptible or incorruptible. Every nature, therefore, is good. I use the word "nature" for the more usual word "substance." Every substance, therefore, is either God or from God, since every good is either God or from God.[1]   128

Now that these points have been firmly established at the head, as it were, of our argumentation, pay attention to what I say next. Every rational nature endowed with free choice of the will is, without doubt, to be praised if it continues to enjoy the highest and immutable Good. Also, every nature which tries to continue to enjoy the highest and immutable Good is to be praised. Every nature, however, which does not continue, or does not will to act in such a way as to continue to enjoy the highest, immutable Good, is to be blamed insofar as it fails either to continue or to act so that it may continue to enjoy this. If, therefore, the rational nature which has been created is praised, no one doubts that its Creator should be praised, and if it is blamed, no one doubts that its Creator is being praised even as it is blamed. In addition, when we blame the rational nature because it does not will to enjoy the highest and immutable Good which is its own Creator, without a doubt we are praising the Creator. How great is that Good! How impossible to express in language or thought is the praise and honor we owe to God, the Creator of all! For unless we praise Him, we cannot be praised or blamed! For we cannot be blamed for not continuing to enjoy   129   130   131

---

[1] In the previous and subsequent sections, the translation "nature" is reserved for cases in which Augustine uses the term *natura*. In spite of his identification of nature (*natura*) with substance (*substantia*), it will be observed that replacement of the former term, wherever it occurs, by the latter leads to logical awkwardnesses. Augustine appears to have conflated, in the term *natura*, the notions of substance, as existing individual or particular, and of essence, as the proper or normative *form* of a class of individuals.

this Good unless abiding in It is the great, highest, and foremost Good for us. How can this be true unless that inexpressible Good is God? What, then, can be found in our sins that we should blame God! There is no blame for our sins unless He is praised.

132   When we blame things, what else do we blame in them except imperfection? Moreover, we blame no thing's imperfection without giving praise to the nature which has the imperfection. For either what you blame is according to the nature of the thing, and is not an imperfection (you should therefore be corrected so that you may know how to blame correctly!); or, if there is an imperfection which can rightly be blamed, it must be contrary to the thing's very nature.

133   Indeed, every imperfection, by the very fact it is an imperfection, is contrary to nature, indeed, to the nature of the very thing of which it is an imperfection. If it does not harm the nature, then it is not an imperfection. However, if it is an imperfection because it spoils the nature, it is an imperfection because it is contrary to the nature. But if a nature is corrupted by another's imperfection and not by its own, it is unjustly blamed, and we must ask whether the nature which was able to corrupt the other was corrupted through its own imperfection. For what is it for something to be spoiled, if

134   not to be corrupted through an imperfection? Furthermore, the uncorrupted nature is without imperfection, but the nature whose imperfection corrupts another nature is certainly itself imperfect. Therefore, the nature which can corrupt another is already full of imperfection and has been previously corrupted through its own imperfection. From this it follows that every imperfection is contrary to the nature even of that very thing of which it is an imperfection. Therefore, since nothing is blamed in a thing except imperfection, and since it is an imperfection because it is contrary to the nature of the thing of which it is an imperfection, nothing can properly be blamed without praising the nature. For what rightly displeases you in the imperfection is simply that it spoils what pleases you in the nature.

XIV.
Not all forms of corruption are attributable to imperfection.

A.   We should also investigate the following question: 135
Is it correct to say that a nature can be corrupted by the imperfection of another without its also having some imperfection of its own? For if the nature which comes with its own
imperfection to corrupt another does not find something corruptible in the other, it does not cause corruption. If, however, it finds something corruptible, it adds its own imperfection and causes corruption. If the stronger is unwilling to
be corrupted by the weaker, then it is not corrupted. If, however, it is willing, it begins to be corrupted by its own imperfection even before being corrupted by the other's. An
equal cannot be corrupted by an equal unless it is willing to
be. If an imperfect nature approaches a perfect nature, it does 136
not approach as an equal, but is weaker because of its imperfection. Indeed, if a stronger nature corrupts a weaker, the
corruption is due either to the imperfection of the other (if it
comes about because of the depraved desire of both) or to
the imperfection of the stronger (if the nature is so outstanding that, though full of imperfection, it is yet stronger than
the weaker which it corrupts). Who would rightly blame the 137
fruits of the earth because imperfect men spoil them by mis-
using them for extravagances? Yet it would be the mark of a
madman to doubt that the nature of man, even when full of
imperfections, is nobler and stronger than the unspoiled
fruits of the earth. If we define imperfection as "that which 138
deserves blame," it can happen that a stronger nature may
corrupt a weaker one, and that this may come about through
no imperfection on the part of either. For example, who
would dare blame the frugal man who seeks nothing else
from the fruits of the earth except the necessities of his nature, or who corrupts the fruits of the earth by using them
for food? Such corruption by use is not really even called cor-

139 ruption, since the word "corruption" usually implies imperfection. It can easily be seen in other cases that, in the
course of fulfilling its needs, a stronger nature generally corrupts a weaker one, either because of the order of justice
when it punishes a fault [culpa]—from which has come the
rule spoken by the Apostle, "If any man spoils the temple
of God, God spoils him" [1]—or in accord with the order of
mutable things which yield to him according to the most fitting laws which have been given for the well-being of each
140 part of the universe. If the sun by its brightness should harm
someone's eyes that are too weak because of the limits of their
nature to bear the light, we must not think that the sun
should change the eyes so that they can then satisfy their
desire for the sun's light, or that this happened because of an
imperfection in the sun. Least of all should the eyes themselves be blamed, because they yielded to their master and
141 opened to the light, so that the light ruined them. Of all of
the types of corruption, therefore, only the corruption that
is full of imperfection is rightly blamed. There are other
kinds not even to be called corruption, which are surely not
full of imperfection and cannot be worthy of blame. The
word "blame," because it has been made up for (that is, is
fitted and proper to) imperfection, is believed to have been
derived from the word for imperfection [vitium] and is thus
called "blame" [vituperatio].
142   An imperfection, as I began to say, is not evil for any other
reason than that it is opposed to the nature of the very thing
of which it is an imperfection. From this it is evident that the
same object which has a blameworthy imperfection is a praiseworthy nature, so that we admit that blaming imperfections
is praising the natures which have the blameworthy imperfections. Since an imperfection is opposed to the nature, the
degree to which the imperfection is evil is equal to the
amount by which the completeness of the nature is decreased.
143 Therefore, when you blame an imperfection, are you not
really praising that in which you desire completeness? And

[1] I Cor. 3:17.

to what does this completeness belong except to the nature?
A perfect nature does not deserve any blame; instead it deserves praise in its own kind. Therefore, whatever you observe
to be lacking to the perfection of a nature, you call an imperfection, and in so doing you testify that the nature is pleasing
to you which you would wish to be perfect as you blame its
incompleteness.

XV.
Not all imperfections in creatures are worthy
of blame.

A. If, therefore, by blaming imperfections we suggest   144
the beauty and worth of the very natures which possess imperfections, how much more should we praise God, the Creator of all natures even in their imperfections! For to God they
owe the fact that they are natures. Their imperfection is as
great as the distance they have gone from the design by which
God made them. When we blame them, we do so in terms
of the design by which we see they were made; thus, we blame
them for what we do not see in them. And if the very design   145
through which all things were made (namely, the highest and
immutable Wisdom of God) truly exists in the highest degree
—and indeed it does—see what may become of whatever de-
parts from the design.

Nevertheless, this defect would not deserve blame if it were
not voluntary. Listen then, please: are you right to blame
what is as it ought to be? I think not. Yet you are right to
blame what is not as it ought to be. No one owes what he
has not received. And to whom does the debtor owe, if not to
him from whom he has received? The debts which are re-   146
turned in a bequest are returned to the man who made the
bequest. Any credit returned to the rightful heirs is paid to
those who succeed by that right; otherwise it would not be
a payment but only a release or surrender, or something of
the sort. Therefore, it is foolish for us to say that temporal
objects ought not to pass away. They have been placed in

the order of the universe in such a way that, unless they do pass away, future objects cannot succeed to past ones, and only thus can the whole beauty of times past, present, and 147   future be accomplished in their own kind. They use what they have received and return it to Him to whom they owe their existence and greatness. The man who grieves that these things pass away ought to listen to his own speech, to see if he thinks the complaint that he makes is just and proceeds from prudence. If someone likes the least bit of the complaint that comes to his ears and does not want it to pass on and yield its place, so that the whole complaint may be made by passing and succeeding parts, he will be judged quite mad!

148   Therefore, in the case of objects which pass away because they have been granted only a limited existence in order that everything may be accomplished in its time, no one is right to blame this deficiency. No one can say, "It ought to re-149   main," when it cannot pass the accepted limits. Moreover, in the case of rational creatures (in whom, whether they sin or not, the beauty of the universe finds its fullest expression), either there are no sins—which is a most foolish thing to say, for he sins who condemns things as sins which are not sins; or else sins are not to be blamed—which is no less foolish. For then, either things wrongly made will begin to receive praise, and the whole attention of the human mind will be disturbed and will upset life; or else the deed which has been done as it ought to have been done will be blamed, and accursed madness will result—or, to speak more mildly, a 150   wretched error. If truest reason forces us to blame sins, and whatever is rightly blamed is blamed because it is not as it ought to be, ask what a sinful nature owes and you will find the answer, "right action" [recte factum]. Ask to whom it owes this and you will find the answer, "to God." For from God the rational nature received the possibility of acting rightly when it so willed; from God, too, comes the fact that it is unhappy if it has not acted rightly, and happy if it has acted rightly.

151   Since no one is above the laws of the omnipotent Creator,

the soul is not allowed not to repay what it owes. Either it repays what it received by using it rightly, or else it repays the debt by forfeiting what it is not willing to use well. If the soul does not pay its debt by doing justice, it will pay its debt by enduring unhappiness—the word "debt" is applicable in either case. We can express what we have said in the following way: If a man does not pay his debt by doing what he ought, he pays it by suffering what he ought. These are not 152 separated by any interval of time, however, so that a man at one time does not do what he ought and at some other time suffer what he ought. The universal beauty is not marred by time. Thus, the ugliness of sin is never without the beauty of punishment. But all that is now secretly punished will be disclosed, with all its bitter unhappiness, in the judgment to come. Just as anyone who is not awake is asleep, so anyone 153 who does not do what he ought suffers at once what he ought, because there is such great beauty in justice that no one can escape from it, except into unhappiness. In every case of deficiency, therefore, either the natures have not received what they lack and thus there is no sin (just as while they exist there is no sin since they have not received more than they are); or they are unwilling to be what, if they were willing, they could be, and because the nature that they received is good, they are punished if they are unwilling to fulfill that nature.

XVI.
God is not responsible for human sin.

A.   But God owes nothing to anyone, for He freely main- 154 tains the universe. Even if someone should say that God owes him something for his merits, surely God is under no obligation for having given the man existence; it is not to the man that something is owing. Besides, what is the merit in turning to God, from whom you have your existence, since you do so to better yourself through Him who gave you your existence? What then do you ask—as if you were demanding pay-

ment of a debt? If you do not will to turn to Him, what loss
is it to God? It is your loss, for you would be nothing without Him who made you something. Unless you turn to Him
and repay the existence that He gave you, you won't be
155 "nothing"; you will be wretched. All things owe to God, first
of all, what they are insofar as they are natures. Then, those
who have received a will owe to Him whatever better thing
they can will to be, and whatever they ought to be. No man
is ever blamed for what he has not been given, but he is
justly blamed if he has not done what he should have done;
and if he has received free will and sufficient power, he stands
156 under obligation. When a man does not do what he ought,
God the Creator is not at fault. It is to His glory that a man
suffers justly; and by blaming a man for not doing what he
should have done, you are praising what he ought to do. You
are praised for seeing what you ought to do, even though you
see this only through God, who is immutable Truth; how
much more, then, should God be praised, since He has taught
you to will, has given you the power to will, and has not
157 allowed unwillingness to go unpunished! If every man owes
what he has received, and if man was made so that he must
necessarily sin, then he is obliged to sin. Therefore, when he
sins, he does what he ought. But if it is wicked to say this,
then no one is forced to sin by his own nature; nor is he
forced to sin by any other nature. Indeed, no one sins when
158 he suffers what he has not willed. If he suffers justly, his sin
lies, not in the fact that he suffers unwillingly, but in the fact
that he willingly acted in such a way as to suffer justly what
he did not will. If he suffers unjustly, how does he sin? For
to sin is not to suffer something unjustly, but to do something unjust. But if no one is forced to sin, either by his
own nature or by that of another, it follows that he sins of his
159 own will. If you wish to attribute his sin to the Creator, you
will acquit the sinner of his sin. If the sinner is rightly defended, he has not sinned, and there is nothing to be imputed
to the Creator. Let us, therefore, praise the Creator if the
sinner can be defended, and let us praise Him if he cannot.
For if he is justly defended, he is not a sinner—therefore,

praise the Creator. If he cannot be defended, he is a sinner insofar as he has turned away from his Creator—therefore, praise the Creator.

I cannot find, and I assert that there cannot be found, any 160 way in which to attribute our sins to God the Creator. I find that He is to be praised in these very sins, because He punishes them and because they occur when we turn from His truth.

E. I willingly accept and approve, and I agree that our sins cannot properly be attributed to our Creator.

XVII.
The will is the radical cause of all evil.

E. But I would nevertheless like to know, if I can, why 161 that nature which God foreknows will not sin, does not sin; and why that other nature which God foreknows will sin, does so. For I no longer think it is because God's foreknowledge compels the latter to sin and the former not to. Yet if 162 there were no cause, the rational creature could not be divided into three types: one that never sins, and one that always sins, and one in between, that sometimes sins and sometimes acts rightly. What cause made these three divisions? I 163 will not accept the answer "the will," because I am asking for the cause of the will itself. It is not without cause that, although all are of the same class, the first will never wills to sin, the second always wills to sin, and the last sometimes wills to sin and sometimes does not. I clearly understand that the threefold division is not without cause, but what the cause may be I do not know.[1]

A. Since the will is the cause of sin and you are asking 164 for the cause of the will itself, if I can find the cause, won't you then ask what is the cause of the cause that I just revealed? Will there be any end to your questions, delays, and postponements, when you really should want no more than to know the root of the question? Beware lest you think that 165 anything could be more true than the words, "The root of all

---

[1] This is the last time Evodius enters the dialogue.

evil is avarice." [2] Don't will to have more than is sufficient, and "sufficient" means the amount that a nature needs to

166 maintain itself in its own kind. For avarice, which the Greeks call *philargyria* [love of money]—the word is probably derived from the fact that the ancients used coins made of silver and alloys of silver—is to be understood not only as love of money or coins, but also as any sort of love in which one has immoderate desire and wants more than is enough. This avarice

167 is desire, and desire is a wicked will. Therefore, a wicked will is the cause of all evil. If the will were in accord with its nature, it would surely maintain that nature, not harm it; and therefore, it would not be wicked. From this we gather that the root of evil is this: not being in accord with nature. This is a sufficient explanation for those who wish to accuse natures [of being the cause of evil]. How could it be the root of all evil, if you ask for its cause? Instead, the root would be whatever caused it, and your questions would have no end.

168 After all, what cause of the will could there be, except the will itself? It is either the will itself, and it is not possible to go back to the root of the will; or else it is not the will, and there is no sin. Either the will is the first cause of sin, or else there is no first cause. Sin cannot rightly be imputed to any-

169 one but the sinner, nor can it rightly be imputed to him unless he wills it. I do not know why you ask anything else. Finally, whatever may be the cause of will, it is certainly either just or unjust. If it is just, he who obeys it does not sin; if unjust, he who does not obey it does not sin.

XVIII.
Is an act sinful if it could, by virtue of man's ignorance and difficulty, not be avoided?

170 *A.* Is it violence, perhaps, that compels a man against his will? How many times must we repeat the same thing? Remember everything we said earlier about sin and free will. But if it is too much trouble to commit them all to memory,

[2] I Tim. 6:10.

remember the following, which is very short: whatever be the cause of will, if it cannot be resisted, it is no sin to yield to it. If it can be resisted, and a man does not yield to it, he does not sin. If it deceive the uncautious man, then beware of 171 deception. If it be so deceptive that it cannot be guarded against, then there are no sins; for who commits sin when he cannot defend himself against it? But men do sin; therefore, sin can be avoided.

Yet even certain things done in ignorance are blamed and 172 judged to need correction, as we read in the Holy Scriptures where the Apostle says, "I obtained mercy because I acted in ignorance," [1] and the prophet, "Remember not the deeds of my youth and ignorance." [2] There are acts done by necessity that are to be blamed where the man willed to act rightly and could not. For whence are these words, "For I do not 173 the good which I will to do and I do the evil which I hate?" [3] And this: "To will is present with me; to accomplish that which is good I find not." [4] And this: "For the flesh lusts against the spirit and the spirit against the flesh. For these things are contrary to one another, so that you do not the things you will." [5] But all these things are characteristic of men who have come from the damnation of death; for if it is not the punishment of man, but his nature, then these things are not sins. If a man does not depart from the way he 174 was made by nature—and the order of the universe cannot be improved on—he does what he ought when he does these things. If man were good, he would be other than as he is. Now, however, since he is as he is, he is not good, and does not have it in his power to be good—either because he does not see what he ought to be, or because he does see, yet does not have the power to be what he sees he ought to be. Who 175

1 I Tim. 1:13.
2 Ps. 24:7 (Ps. 26:7).
3 Rom. 7:15, 19.
4 Rom. 7:18.
5 Gal. 5:17.

would doubt that this is a punishment? Every penalty that is just is a penalty for sin, and is called punishment. If, however, it is an unjust penalty, since no one doubts that it is a penalty, it is imposed on man by some unjust ruler. Since only a madman would doubt the omnipotence or justice of

176 God, the penalty is just and is a penalty for some sin. For no unjust ruler could steal man away from God without God's knowledge, or wrest him away against God's will (as if God were too weak, or could be terrified or frightened!) in order to torture man with an unjust penalty. It follows, therefore, that this just penalty comes from man's condemnation.

177 We should not be amazed that, because of his ignorance, man has not free choice of will to choose what he should rightly do. We should not wonder that a man may see what he ought to do and may will to do it, yet he cannot, through the resistance of carnal habit—which is, as it were, naturally increased by that violence which his mortality has bequeathed

178 him. It is an absolutely just punishment for sin that each man loses what he is unwilling to use rightly, when he could without any difficulty use it if he willed. Thus the man who does not act rightly although he knows what he ought to do, loses the power to know that is right; and whoever is unwilling to do right when he can, loses the power to do it when he wills to. In fact, two penalties—ignorance and difficulty—beset every sinful soul. Through ignorance, the soul is disgraced

179 by error. Through difficulty, it is tormented by pain. The approval of false things as true, so that man makes a wrong judgment against his will, and the lack of power to abstain from lust because of the opposition and torments of the bondage of the flesh—these two things are not in the nature of man as he was made, but are the penalties of man who has been condemned. When we speak of the will that is free to do right, we speak of the will with which man was [first] made.

XIX.
The sin of Adam, inherited by sinners, cannot be admitted as an excuse for their ignorance and difficulty.

A.   At this point, there arises a question often wrangled 180
over by those discontented men who are ready to blame anything whatsoever—except themselves—for sin. For they say,
"If Adam and Eve sinned, what did we, poor wretches, do?
Why should we be born with the blindness of ignorance and
the tortures of difficulty? Why should we first wander about,
ignorant of what we should do, then, when the teachings of
justice begin to be disclosed to us, why should we will to do
the right things and yet, prevented by some sort of carnal
desire, be unable to do them?" Our reply to these men is 181
brief: let them be silent, and cease to murmur against God.
They might, perhaps, have a valid complaint if there were
no Victor over error and lust. Although there is One present
everywhere who in many ways through His creation beckons
to hostile servants, instructs believers, comforts those who
hope, encourages those who work, aids those who try, and
hears those who pray, you are not considered at fault if you,
against your will, are ignorant; however, if you are ignorant
because you fail to ask, you are at fault. You are not blamed
because you do not bind up your wounded limbs. Your sin
is that you despise Him who wishes to heal you. No one is 182
denied the knowledge of how to seek advantageously what,
to his disadvantage, he does not know, and how he must
humbly confess his stupidity, so that He who neither errs or
toils when he comes to give aid may help the man who seeks
and confesses. What a man through ignorance does not do 183
rightly, and what he cannot do, even though he wills rightly,
are called sins because their origin lies in free will. His previous deeds merited these consequences. Just as we speak of a 184
tongue not only as a member which moves in the mouth
while we speak, but also as that which proceeds from the

movement of the member, that is, the form and sound of words according to which we say, "This is Latin" or "That is Greek"; so we call sin not only what is properly called sin because it is committed from free will and in full knowledge, but even that which must follow from the punishment of sin.

185   Thus we speak of nature in one way when we refer to man's nature as he was first created, faultless in his own class; and we speak of it in another way when we refer to the nature into which, as a result of the penalty of condemnation, we were born mortal, ignorant, and enslaved by the flesh. Of this the Apostle says, "We also were by nature the children of wrath, as were the others." [1]

XX.

However souls may come into the world, it is not unjust that the descendants of Adam should inherit the punishment of ignorance and difficulty imposed upon Adam.

186   *A.*   God, the highest Ruler of the universe, justly decreed that we, who are descended from that first union, should be born into ignorance and difficulty, and be subject to death, because they sinned and were hurled headlong into the midst of error, difficulty, and death. God the Ruler of the universe justly resolved this, that the justice of punishment might be made apparent through man's birth, and that the mercy of freeing man from sin might become apparent as man progressed. For happiness was not so taken away from the first man in his condemnation that he was deprived of fruitfulness. He was able, through his offspring, although born of flesh and mortal, to become an honor to his own class and an

187   ornament of the earth. It was not just for man to beget offspring better than himself. The willing man should not only not be hindered, but even be aided in overcoming, through conversion to God, the punishment which his origin merited because of its having turned from God. In this way, the Creator of the universe has shown how easily man could, if he

1 Eph. 2:3.

willed, have remained as he was created, since his descendants
could rise above their birth. Then, if one soul was created   188
from which are derived the souls of all who are born, who
can say that he has not sinned when the original soul sinned?
If, on the other hand, each man's soul is created individually
as he is born, it is not wrong—indeed, it appears most suitable
in accord with the order of the universe—that the evil of the
former soul should be in the nature of the later one, and the
good of the later be in the nature of the former.

Why is it unsuitable if the Creator wanted to show how   189
far the worth of the soul surpasses the worth of corporeal
creatures, so that the corporeal creature can rise only up to
the grade from which the soul has fallen? When the sinful
soul comes upon ignorance and difficulty, it is right to say
that this is a punishment, since before this punishment the
soul was better. If, therefore, a soul should start out—before   190
it has sinned or has even been alive—in the state that another soul was in after a blameworthy life, it still possesses no
small amount of good. Therefore, it owes thanks to its Creator, because at its birth and beginning it is still better than
any corporeal object, even a perfect one. The soul is not a
mere intermediate good, not only because it is a soul and by
its very nature surpasses every corporeal object, but also
because it has means of educating itself with the help of its
Creator and can, by pious zeal, acquire and possess all the
virtues through which it can be freed of torturous difficulty
and blinding ignorance. If this is the case, ignorance and diffi-   191
culty will not be the punishment of sin for souls as they
were born, but will be the encouragement for advancement
and the beginning of perfection. It is no trifling matter that
even before the merit of good works, the soul has received a
natural power of judgment [naturale judicium] by which it
prefers wisdom to error and peace to difficulty, so that it
achieves these not simply by being born, but instead by its
own endeavor. If the soul is not willing to act, it may justly
be regarded as guilty of sin, for it has not put to good use the
faculty that it received. For although it was born in igno-   192
rance and difficulty, nevertheless it is not compelled by neces-

sity to remain in the state in which it was born. Absolutely no one except Almightly God could have been the Creator of such souls, which He created even before He was loved by them, and which He perfects when they love Him. Before they exist, God ordains their existence; when they love the Cause of their existence, He ordains their happiness.

193   If already existing souls are sent forth from some secret place in God's world to animate and rule the bodies of each individual who is born, they are sent so that the body, even though it was born of the punishment of sin—that is, the mortality of the first man—might prepare itself, in due order and at the proper time, for the place of heavenly incorruption. It does so by being well controlled, that is, by being purified by virtue and submitting to the rightful servitude

194   ordained of God's creation. When these souls enter into this life and put on the mortal body, they must forget their former life and undergo the hardships of the present one. Thus result ignorance and difficulty, which are the first man's penalty of mortality, imposed to expiate the wretchedness of the spirit; but they are also the spirit's door to restoring the body's in-

195   corruption. They are sins only in the sense that the flesh, which comes from the seed of a sinner, creates ignorance and difficulty for the soul that enters it. Ignorance and difficulty are not faults to be attributed either to the soul or to its

196   Creator. God gave to the soul the power of good works for duties that are toilsome; He gave it the way to faith for the blindness caused by forgetfulness. He also gave to every soul the power of judgment, by which it affirms that it must seek what, to its disadvantage, it does not know; that it must struggle patiently amidst toilsome duties, to overcome the difficulty of right action; and that it must beg the Creator for help in its endeavor. It is God who counsels man to endeavor, outwardly by His law and inwardly by speaking to the very depths of the heart. He prepares the glory of a blessed city for those that triumph over the one who conquered the first man by evil persuasion, and led him to wretchedness. Men afterwards take on this wretchedness in order to conquer him by firmest

197   faith. It is a battle of no small glory to conquer the devil by

assuming this punishment, which the devil boasts to have brought upon man after conquering him. Whoever, enthralled by the love of this life, neglects his task, will in no way be just to lay blame for his crime of desertion upon the rule of the King. He will, instead, be placed by the Lord of all amidst the ranks of him whose disgraceful pay he cherished enough to desert his own camp.

Assume that souls are formed elsewhere and that, instead 198 of being sent by the Lord God to live in bodies, they come there of their own will. It is easy to see that, whatever ignorance and difficulty may result, this is the soul's own choosing, and the Creator should not be blamed. And even if He Himself sent these souls from which He did not take the free will to seek, to ask, and to try—despite their ignorance and difficulty—He is ready to give to those who ask, to explain to those who seek, and to open to those who knock; therefore, He is utterly beyond blame. He has arranged that, when 199 those who are zealous and of good will overcome ignorance and difficulty, they merit a crown of glory. Yet when they are remiss and wish to defend their sins on the ground of weakness, He does not impose ignorance and difficulty as a penalty for crime. Instead, He justly punishes them because they desire to remain in ignorance and difficulty, and because they are unwilling to arrive at truth and peace through zealously seeking and learning, and humbly confessing and praying.

XXI.

Since at present we lack the knowledge or insight to discover the truth about how the soul comes into the world, we must guard against accepting blindly anything which would falsely deceive us about our Creator.

A. There are these four theories concerning the soul: 200 [1] The soul comes from propagation. [2] The soul is created new in the case of every individual. [3] The soul exists elsewhere and is sent divinely into the body of a man at birth;

or lastly [4] of its own will, it slips into bodies. We must not affirm any one of these rashly. Either the catholic commentaries on the divine Scriptures have not yet given this question the explanation and enlightenment that its obscurity and complexity deserve; or, if it has already been done, the book

201   has not reached my hands. May our faith be so great that there is nothing false or unworthy of being felt about the nature of the Creator! In our journey of devotion, our goal is God. If therefore we think of Him otherwise than as He is, our thinking compels us to walk in vanity, not in blessedness; but if we think something false about creation, as long as we do not mistake our opinion for known fact, there is no danger.

202   To attain blessedness, we should not set our course toward a creature, but toward the Creator Himself. If we are persuaded anything that is wrong or untrue about the Creator, we are being deceived by a most pernicious error. No one can come to the blessed life by going toward something that either does

203   not exist, or does not cause blessedness. In order to contemplate the eternal truth and be able to enjoy and cling to it, a road has been provided for us so that we, despite our weakness, may escape from what is temporal. Thus, so far as is sufficient for our journey toward the eternal, we may trust in the past and future—a doctrine of faith which is governed by divine mercy, and so has powerful authority. The present, however, insofar as it pertains to a creature, is perceived as something transitory, through the mutability and inconstancy of body and spirit. We are not able to keep in our

204   cognition what we do not experience in the present. Therefore, whatever things, past or future, we are told on divine authority concerning creation are to be believed. Even though some of them have passed by before we could perceive them, and some have not yet reached our senses, nevertheless they are of the greatest value in strengthening our hope and encouraging our devotion; therefore they are to be believed without any doubt, as long as they procure us our deliverance through the most perfectly ordered temporal sequence which God oversees.

Any error that assumes the guise of divine authority is re- 205
futed chiefly by the following reasoning: it is an error, if it is
shown to affirm or maintain either that there is any mutable
form apart from God's creation, or that there is any mutable
form within the substance of God, or if it asserts of the divine substance that it is either more or less than the Trinity.
All Christian vigilance is bent upon the pious and thoughtful
understanding of the Trinity, and this understanding is the
goal of all our progress. But this is not the place to discuss the 206
unity and equality of the Trinity, or the distinctive nature
of each of its Persons. It is easy—and people do it often—to
mention the doctrines about our Lord God, Author, Builder,
and Ordainer of the universe—doctrines which are part of a
firm faith, and which aid our purpose when, weak as a suck-
ling babe, it is just beginning to raise itself from earthly
to heavenly things. To treat the whole question thoroughly, 207
however, dealing with it so that every man's intelligence may
be convinced by clear reasoning, insofar as is permitted in
this life, cannot seem to be undertaken conveniently or easily
by the eloquence or reason of any man, let alone mine.

Let us, therefore, proceed as we began, insofar as we are 208
aided and allowed: whatever past or future events are told
us concerning the creation are to be believed without doubt,
if they are capable of drawing us toward perfect religion by
arousing us to the sincerest love of God and neighbor. Against 209
unbelievers, however, these facts must be defended so that
faithlessness may be crushed by the weight of authority and
they may be shown, as far as possible, first, how it is not
stupid to believe such things, and secondly, how it is stupid
not to believe them. Nevertheless, we must refute false doctrine not so much when it concerns the past and future as
when it concerns the present, and particularly when it concerns immutable things. As far as we can, we should prove
our position with clear reasoning.

Within the temporal sequence, the anticipation of the 210
future is clearly to be preferred to the search into the past.
Even in the divine Scriptures the past events which are re-

counted bear the prefiguration or promise or testimony of
the future. Indeed, in the things, both good and bad, that
concern this life, what a man has done is not the object of
concern. Instead, all our ardent anxiety is turned upon the
211   future that man anticipates. In times of happiness or of sad-
ness, whatever has befallen us in the past, because it has
passed, is thought of by some kind of inner feeling as if it had
never occurred. What does it matter to me if I do not know
when I began to exist, since I know that I now exist and
believe hopefully in my future existence? I do not trouble myself about my past, and, if my judgment about past events
is mistaken, I do not take this error to be serious. Instead,
with the mercy of my Creator as my guide, I direct my course
212   toward what I shall be. If, therefore, I believe or think something that is not true about what I shall be or with whom I
shall be, this is a serious error, one that I must avoid lest I
fail to make the necessary preparations, or be unable to arrive
at the goal I proposed, as long as I confuse truth with falsity.
Therefore, just as, in preparing my clothing, it does not matter to me if I forget the cold that is past, but it does matter
if I think that no cold spell threatens in the future, so it does
not matter to my soul if it forgets what it has experienced by
chance, so long as it carefully turns toward what it has been
213   advised to prepare, and holds on to it. For example, there is
no harm for the man sailing to Rome to forget what shore he
sailed from, as long as he knows where to direct his boat from
the place where he is. It does him no good to remember the
shore he set sail from, if he is wrecked upon a reef because he
had a mistaken idea about the port of Rome. In the same
way, it is not harmful to me if I do not retain the beginning
of my span of life, as long as I know where I shall rest. The
memory of the beginning of my life, or conjecture about it,
is of no profit to me, if I fall upon the rocks of error because
I think something that is not worthy about God Himself,
who is the one End of the soul's striving.

214   I do not intend this discussion to cause anyone to think
that we forbid that he who is able should examine, with the

help of the divinely inspired Scriptures, whether a soul is
propagated by a soul, or whether each soul is created for an
individual body, or whether, at divine will, they are sent from
somewhere to rule and animate a body, or whether they enter
bodies of their own will. We do not forbid this, if the reasoning of a question which must be solved demands that one
consider and discuss these four points, or if leisure from
more necessary matters allows them to be examined and
treated. Rather, I would say this: A man should not become   215
incensed if another man does not accept his view concerning
the origin of souls. If a man understands something clearly
and surely, let him not think that another man has lost hope
of the things to come because he does not recall the begin-
nings of things past.

XXII.
Even if ignorance and difficulty were part of
man's nature, God is still to be praised.

A.   However the case may stand, whether it should be   216
passed over entirely or put off for further consideration on
another occasion, the present question is not affected, since
it is evident nonetheless that the souls of sinners suffer punishment at the hands of the most perfect, the most just, the
most steadfast and changeless Majesty and Substance of the
Creator. These sins, as we said a while ago, must be attributed only to man's will. We need seek no further cause of
sins.

If ignorance and difficulty are in the nature of man, it is   217
from them that the soul begins to advance and proceed toward knowledge and peace until, through these, the blessed
life is achieved. If, by its own will, the soul fails to make
progress in the highest pursuits and in religious zeal—and
the power to pursue this is not denied to it—the soul is quite
justly hurled headlong into darker ignorance and graver difficulties for punishment, and is placed in a lower order in accordance with a most fitting and proper governance. For the   218

soul is not accountable for the things of which it is ignorant by nature and which, by its nature, it cannot do. But it must be held to account for what it has not tried to know, and for what it has not taken proper care in preparing itself to perform rightly. Not to know how to talk and not to be able to talk is natural for an infant. This ignorance and difficulty of speech in the child hardly deserves blame under the rules of the grammarians; besides, it is pleasant and delightful to human feelings. The infant has not neglected this power, nor has he lost what he once possessed through any fault of his.

219   Therefore, if blessedness for us consisted of fine speech and if it were considered a crime to err in speech and grammar in the same way as when we err in the activities of living, no one would denounce an infant because it set out from this point to pursue eloquence. Clearly, however, a man would rightly be condemned if by the perversity of his will he had either returned to babbling like an infant, or had remained

220   at that first stage. So even now, if ignorance of the truth and difficulty in behaving rightly are the natural points from which man begins his ascent toward the blessedness of wisdom and tranquility, no one properly condemns the soul because of its natural origin. But if a man refuses to strive for excellence, or wills to step back from where he set out, he justly and properly suffers punishment.

221   The Creator of man is in all respects to be praised: whether because from the beginning He instills in man the capacity for the highest good, or because He aids man in attaining this good, or because He completes and perfects man's progress; and He justly ordains [ordinat] the justest condemnation for sinners—either those who, from the first, refuse to strive for achievement, or those who slip back from a higher state—

222   according to their just deserts. Besides, we cannot say that God created an evil soul on the basis of the argument that it is not so great as it has the power to be if it advances, because all the bodily excellences are by far inferior to the soul's very first stage, yet anyone in his right mind judges them praiseworthy in their own class. Thus the soul's ignorance of what it should do arises from the fact that it has

not yet the power to know. It will receive this power, however, if it uses well what it has received. Moreover, it has received the power to search diligently and piously if it wills.
And even when it knows what it must do, it lacks the power
immediately to do so, since the soul has not yet received this
power. For a certain higher part of the soul has advanced   223
already to the point of judging the good of righteous action,
while a slower, carnal part of the soul is not led by reason to
this judgment. Thus, as a result of this very difficulty, the
soul is urged to pray to the One who aids it toward its perfection, whom it recognizes as its Creator. Thus He becomes
dearer to the soul; for, not merely through its own power, but
through the goodness and mercy of Him who is the Source
of its being, it is raised to blessedness. The dearer the Source
of its being becomes to the soul, the more firmly does the soul
rest in Him, and the more richly does it delight in His
eternity. If we would be entirely incorrect in calling the seed-   224
ling and the first growth of a tree sterile, though quite a few
seasons may pass before the tree shows its fruitfulness, why
is not the Author of the soul to be praised with due piety,
since He created the soul in such a way that, with proper
effort and growth, it may bring forth the fruit of knowledge
and justice? Is it not God who has given the soul such worth
that it is within its power to approach beatitude if it will?

XXIII.
How are the pain and suffering of innocents
to be understood?

A.   But the objection that ignorant men usually raise   225
against this argument concerns the death of little children,
and the bodily sufferings with which we have often seen
children afflicted. They say, "Why need the child have been
born, since he died before he did anything of merit in life?
How will he be judged in the judgment to come, since, having
neither acted rightly nor sinned, he has no place, either
among the just or among the sinners?"

My answer to these men is as follows: In view of the en-   226

compassing network of the universe and the whole creation—
a network that is perfectly ordered in time and place, where
not even one leaf of a tree is superfluous—it is not possible to
create a superfluous man. What is clearly superfluous, however, is any inquiry into the reward of someone who has
merited nothing. There is no need to fear that there could be
a neutral condition between right action and sin without
there being a neutral sentence by the Judge between reward
and punishment.

227   Men usually raise problems about this point, as well: What
good is it for children to receive the sacrament of Christ's
Baptism, when they often die before they know anything
about it? In this case it is quite enough to believe piously
and rightly that the child is aided by the faith of those who
228 brought it to be consecrated. The saving authority of the
church provides that each one may realize from this practice
what benefit his faith is to himself, since it can be of use in
aiding others who have not yet gained their own. What good
was the faith of the widow to her son? He did not have faith,
for he was dead, yet his mother's faith aided him to live
again![1] How much more can one's faith take care of a child
that has not been accused of any fault!

229   Some raise a greater and, as it were, more merciful objection, concerning the bodily suffering with which young children are afflicted. Because of their age, they say, children have
committed no sins (assuming that their souls have not committed sin before animating their bodies). Hence they ask:
"What evil have they done that they should suffer so?" But
what reason is there to believe that anyone should be re-
230 warded for innocence before he could do harm? Since God
works some good by correcting adults tortured by the sickness
and death of children who are dear to them, why should this
suffering not occur? When the sufferings of children are over,
it will be as if they had never occurred for those who suffered.
Either the adults on whose account the sufferings occurred
will become better, if they are reformed by temporal troubles

1 Luke 7:11–13.

and choose to live rightly, or else, if because of the hardships of this life they are unwilling to turn their desire toward eternal life, they will have no excuse when they are punished in the judgment to come. Moreover, who knows what faith 231 is practiced or what pity is tested when these children's sufferings break down the hardness of parents? Who knows what reward God reserves in the secret place of his judgment for the children who, though they have not acted rightly, are not, on the other hand, weighed down by sin? For it is not in vain that the Church commends as martyrs the infants who were slaughtered when Herod sought to slay Jesus Christ our Lord.[2]

These superficial questioners and careless students of such 232 issues, these loquacious sophists, are also in the habit of harassing the faith of the less learned even over the sufferings of dumb beasts by saying, "What evil have beasts done that they should suffer such great hardships? What good can they hope to gain by such suffering?" They say and think this 233 because they think wickedly about these problems. They cannot see the highest good—what it is and how great it is—yet they wish everything to be the same as their idea of the highest good. They cannot think of a highest good beyond the highest corporeal objects which, being celestial, are less subject to corruption. Therefore, they demand quite improperly that the bodies of beasts should suffer no death or corruption—as if they were not mortal, although they are of the lowest order, or as if they were evil because celestial bodies are better. But the pain that beasts feel shows the strength of 234 their souls, a strength admirable and praiseworthy in their own class. From this, it become quite apparent how, in ruling and giving life to their bodies, the souls of beasts are seeking unity. What else is this pain except a sense of resistance to division or corruption? Thus it is clearer than daylight how 235 eager the soul is for unity, and how firmly it holds to unity in the completeness of the body. Neither voluntarily nor indifferently, but rather with hostility and opposition, it turns

[2] See Matt. 2:16.

its attention to the suffering of its body, by which it perceives that its unity and completeness are, to its distress, being
236 shattered. Therefore, we would not see how strong was the
desire for unity in lower animate creatures were it not for the
pain suffered by beasts. If this were not apparent, we would
be less mindful than we ought to be of all that has been arranged by the complete, sublime, and ineffable unity of the
237 Creator. Indeed, when piously and carefully regarded, every
kind of creature and every motion falling under the observa-
tion of the human spirit instruct us by their various motions
and conditions, as if in a variety of tongues; crying out
around us, they repeat that the Creator must be acknowledged. There is nothing that feels either pleasure or pain
which does not seek, in unity, the beauty of its own class and
238 the stability of its own nature. Of all those creatures that
feel the hurt of pain or the delights of pleasure, there is not
a one that does not acknowledge, by the very fact that it
avoids pain and seeks pleasure, that it shuns destruction and
seeks unity. In rational spirits themselves, every desire for
knowledge, in which their very nature rejoices, imposes a
unity upon all that they perceive; and when they err, they flee
from the confusion of incomprehensible ambiguity. Where
does this troublesome ambiguity come from, if not from the
239 lack of complete unity? From this it is clear that everything,
either when it offends or is offended, or else when it delights
or is delighted, suggests and declares the unity of the Creator.
But if ignorance and difficulty, by which this life must begin,
are not in the spirits' very nature, it follows that they should
be undertaken as a duty or imposed as a punishment. I think
now that there has been enough discussion on this problem.

XXIV.
How did the first man fall into folly and ignorance?

240   *A.*   We must inquire into the question of what the first
man was like, rather than how his descendants were conceived. Some people think themselves very clever when they

propose the following question: "If the first man was created wise, then why did he allow himself to be seduced? But if, however, he was created as a stupid fellow, then why isn't God the author of vices, since folly is the greatest of vices?" As if there were not, indeed, some intermediate condition 241 which could properly be called neither wisdom nor folly! A man begins to be either foolish or wise, so that he is of necessity called one or the other, at the time when—unless he is so negligent that his will becomes guilty of vicious folly—he is capable of acquiring wisdom. Just as it is senseless to call 242 an infant stupid, so it would be even more absurd to call it wise, even though it is already a human being. It clearly follows from this that the nature of man allows for some intermediate condition, which cannot rightly be called either wisdom or folly. Thus if someone were born into that same condition in which we find men who lack wisdom through neglect, no one would rightly speak of him as foolish, since the fault lies in his nature rather than in his own wrongdoing. Folly is not just any form of ignorance about what 243 to seek and what to avoid, but rather a vicious ignorance. We do not speak of an irrational animal as stupid because it does not have the power of becoming wise. Yet we often improperly call things "foolish" because of certain resemblances. Likewise, though blindness is a most serious defect of the eyes, it is no defect in newborn animals, and it is not proper to speak of "blindness" in this context.

If, therefore, a man is so created that, although he is not 244 yet wise, he is able to understand a command which he obviously ought to obey, it is no wonder that he could be seduced. It is not unjust that he should suffer punishment when he did not obey the command. Nor is his Creator the author of his sins, for it was not yet man's fault that he was not wise, since he had not received the power to achieve wisdom. Nev- 245 ertheless, he did possess something by which he could have achieved the possession of that which he did not have, if only he had rightly willed to do so. It is one thing to be rational (that is, to be capable of thought), and another to

be wise. Through reason, everyone is capable of compre-
hending a command, obedience to which is the first duty of
246 faith, so that he can do what he is commanded to do. Just
as it is the nature of reason to understand a command, so
it is the nature of wisdom to obey it. Whatever may be the
nature of that faculty that can understand commands, it is
the will which carries them out. Just as the importance of a
rational nature lies in its capacity to receive commands, so
the value of obeying commands lies in the wisdom thereby
received. When a man begins to be able to understand commands, then he begins to be able to sin. There are two ways
in which a man can sin before he has attained wisdom: [1]
he may not have prepared himself to receive a command, or
247 [2] when he has received it, he may not carry it out. But a
wise man sins when he turns aside from wisdom. Just as a
command does not issue from the man who is subject to the
command, but from the one who commands, so also wisdom
does not have its source in the man who is enlightened, but
in Him who enlightens. Therefore, why should not the Crea-
248 tor of man be praised? For man as a being is good; he is
better than beasts because he is able to apprehend a command. He is better still when he has accepted a command,
and again better when he has obeyed it. And he is above all
superior when he has been blessed with the eternal light
of wisdom. The evil of sin, however, is to be found in negligence, either in the acceptance of a command or in its obser-
vation, or in negligence of the continual contemplation of
249 wisdom. From this we can understand how the first man could
have been seduced, although he was created wise. Since this
sin followed from free will, punishment resulted as a just
consequence by divine law. Thus the Apostle Paul says,
"Saying that they are wise, they are made foolish." [1] For pride
turns men away from wisdom, and folly results from this
turning away. Folly is like blindness, as Paul says: "And their
250 foolish heart was darkened." [2] Whence comes this darkness,

[1] Rom. 1:22.
[2] Rom. 1:21.

except from turning away from the light of wisdom? Whence comes this turning away, unless man, to whom God is the Good, replaces God with himself to be his own good, as God is the Good to Himself? Thus it is said, "To me myself, my soul is troubled," [3] and "Taste, and you will be as gods." [4]

The following question, moreover, troubles those who con- 251 sider it: "Was it by folly that the first man departed from God, or was the first man made foolish by his departure from God?" This is troublesome, because if you answer that it was by his folly that he departed from wisdom, it appears that he was subject to folly before he departed from wisdom, so that his folly was the cause of his departure. Likewise, if you reply that he became subject to folly by departing from God, they will inquire whether it was through folly or through wisdom that he departed. "If he acted wisely, then he acted properly and committed no sin at all. If, however, he did what he did subject to folly, then," they argue, "he was already in that state of folly at which he is supposed to have arrived by his departure from God. Had he not already been subject to folly, he could not have committed foolish acts." From this it appears that there must be some intermediate state 252 through which a transition is made from wisdom to folly, a state to which it is impossible to ascribe either wisdom or folly. This intermediate state cannot be understood in this life by men, except through contraries. Thus, no mortal may become 253 wise unless he passes from foolishness to wisdom. If the passage itself is foolishly made, it is not well done—but this sounds like senseless talk, for if the transition is wisely made, then the man was already wise before he passed from folly to wisdom. This is no less absurd. From this we may understand that there is an intermediate state which we cannot call by either name. Thus when the first man passed from the citadel of wisdom to folly, the passage itself was neither wise nor foolish. This is similar to sleeping and waking. Sleeping is 254 not the same as going to sleep, and waking is not the same as

[3] Ps. 41:7 (Ps. 42:6).
[4] Gen. 3:5.

being fully awake. There is a passage from one to the other. Yet there is a significant difference: the above examples illustrate actions usually independent of our will, while the approach to wisdom and the departure from it are never made without the involvement of the will, and hence are most justly followed by suitable retribution.

XXV.
What is seen by the rational substance which turns it away from God, toward evil?

255   *A.*   Yet the will is moved to action by what can be seen. And while people have no power over what they see or touch, they do have it in their power either to accept or to reject. Thus we must grant that the spirit is affected by higher and lower perceptions. Hence it is that the rational substance selects from both classes what it wills, and by virtue of its

256   selection achieves misery or blessedness. In the Garden of Eden, for example, the command of God was visible in the higher goods; the suggestion of the serpent through the lower. Man had no power to determine what God should command,

257   nor could he control what the serpent would suggest. But how free man is, how untrammeled by any chains of difficulty, and constituted in the very vigor of wisdom, may be understood from this: even stupid men overcome these enticements and go on to wisdom, even though it is hard to give up the unwholesome sweetness of pernicious habits.

258   We may ask here, "If the things man sees were presented to him by both sides, that is, by God's command and by the suggestion of the serpent, whence came the suggestion to the devil himself that he pursue the counsel of impiety, which caused him to be hurled down from high heaven?" For had he been moved by nothing that he could see or grasp, he could not have elected to do what he did; had something not entered his mind, he would not have turned his purpose to-

259   ward the unspeakable. How did it enter his mind to do the things which changed him from a good angel into the devil

himself? Surely he who wills, wills something; and unless this
something is suggested from without through the body's
senses, or comes into the mind in hidden ways, he cannot
will. We must distinguish, then, between two kinds of things
that can be seen. One originates in the will of a being who
persuades—for example, the devil, through whose persuasion
and man's consent, man sinned. The second arises out of the
influence of his surroundings, the spirit's intention, or the
bodily senses. Everything except the changeless Trinity is 260
subject to the spirit's intention, for the Trinity is subject to
nothing, but rather surpasses all things. First, therefore, the
spirit itself is subject to its own power of cognition, so that
we are aware that we live; then, the body is subject to the
power which moves any member to its proper task when there
is need. Whatever corporeal objects exist are subject to the
physical senses.

The spirit, when it contemplates the highest wisdom— 261
which, since it is changeless, cannot be the same thing as the
spirit—apprehends even its own changeableness and in a sense
penetrates into its own mind. This could not be the case,
were it not that the spirit is different from God and yet
second only to God. Yet the spirit is even nobler when it for- 262
gets itself in its love of the immutable God; or when, in the
depths of its being, it despises itself by comparison with Him.
If, however, it takes the opposite road and is satisfied with
itself, seeking to imitate God in a perverse way, so that it
wills to delight in its own power—if the spirit takes this road,
the more it desires to be greater, the less it becomes. Thus, 263
"Pride is the root of all sin; and the root of pride is apostasy
from God." [1] But to the pride of the devil was added a most
malevolent ill will and envy, so that he prodded man to the
arrogance through which man knew himself to be condemned.
From this, man incurred a punishment that was corrective 264
rather than fatal. So it is that he to whom the devil presented
himself for the imitation of his arrogance is also he to whom
the Lord—through Whom we are promised eternal life—pre-

[1] Ecclus. 10:14–15.

sents Himself for the imitation of His humility. Thus through the offer of Christ's blood as ransom for us, and after labor and unspeakable suffering, we may cling to our Saviour with a love so great, and be so carried away by his brightness, that nothing we see among the lower things can tear us away from the higher vision; and even though something might be suggested to our attention by lower things, the unending condemnation and torment of the devil is sufficient to recall us from temptation.

265   So great is the beauty of justice, so great the joy of eternal light, of the unchangeable Truth and Wisdom, that even though a man were not allowed to remain in its light for longer than a day, yet in comparison with this he would rightly and properly despise a life of innumerable years spent in the de-

266   light of temporal goods. Indeed, the following is neither false nor trivial: "Far better is one day in thy courts than thousands." [2] Yet it is also possible to understand this in another sense, namely that "thousands of days" may be interpreted to represent the transience of time, while the term "one day" represents the immutability of eternity.

267   I do not know whether I have passed over anything that is required to answer your questions as well as the Lord will allow. Yet even if something else occurs to you, the limits of our book force us to draw to a conclusion, and to rest at last from our discussion.

2 Ps. 83:11.

Appendix: RETRACTATIONS

RETRACTATIONS [1]

[*Around 427 Augustine completed two books entitled* Retractationes, *in which he reviewed in chronological order all of his publications—with the exception, of course, of his letters and sermons—for the purpose of reconsidering some of the doctrines he had expressed. In these two books of* Retractationes, *he revised his earlier conceptions within the wider perspective of his mature thought, and defended his doctrines against incorrect interpretations and misunderstandings. The following translates the section in which Augustine reviews* On Free Choice of the Will, *insisting that it cannot be construed to support the heresy of the British monk Pelagius (c. 360–c. 420) and his followers. As the text below indicates, Augustine accused the Pelagians of so emphasizing human freedom and responsibility (Pelagius is said to have insisted, like Kant, "If I ought, then I can") that the activity of God, through grace, became superfluous in the scheme of salvation. Augustine had entered into the Pelagian controversy in 411–12 and was active from that time onward in writing and preaching against Pelagian doctrines. In 431, a year after Augustine's death, the Council of Ephesus pronounced the Pelagian doctrines heretical.—Trs.*]

While we were still in Rome, we wanted to explore and   1
discuss the origin of evil. We discussed the problem in such
a way that thorough and considered reasoning might bring
us, if possible—insofar as, with God's aid, discussion would
allow us—to an understanding of what we already believed
on the basis of divine authority. After careful reasoning and
debate, we concluded that the sole cause of evil lay in the
free choice of the will; therefore, the three books which our

[1] The marginal numbers follow those of the text edited by Pius Knöll, *Retractationum libri duo*, vol. 37 in the *Corpus Scriptorum Ecclesiasticorum Latinorum* (Leipzig, 1902).

discussion produced were entitled *De Libero Arbitrio*. The second and third books I completed, as best I could at the time, in Africa, after I was ordained priest at Hippo Regius.

2   In these books, we discussed so many points that a number of issues arose which I could not resolve, and which required extended discussion at the time. Such issues were postponed, and our reasoning led to the conclusion that we may believe or even know that God ought to be praised, whatever the truth might be about the unresolved questions to which there appeared no true solution from any point of view—or rather from all points of view on the same questions. The discussion was undertaken with an eye to those who deny that free choice of the will is the cause of evil, and who consequently hold that God, since He is the Creator of everything, is to be blamed. These men—they are the Manichees—in their wickedness and error, wish to assert the existence of a certain principle of evil, immutable and co-eternal with God. Since our discourse was directed at these people, the books do not deal with the question of God's grace, by which He so predestines who the elect shall be that He even prepares the wills of those among them who are already making use of their free choice. Consequently when the occasion arose to mention God's grace, it received only passing notice, not the carefully reasoned defense that would have been required were this the main subject of discussion. For it is one thing to inquire into the source of evil, and quite another to inquire how to return to our former good, or even to attain a greater one.

3   Therefore, the recent Pelagian heretics—who maintain a theory of free choice of the will inconsistent with the Grace of God, since they argue that it is given in accordance with our merits—must not boast of my support. Much was said supporting the doctrine of free choice in these books. This was required by the purpose of the discussion. I said, in the first book, "Evil deeds are punished by the justice of God," and I added, "It would not be just to punish evil deeds if they were not done willfully." [2]

2 P. 3, § 3.

Again, when I demonstrated that the good will is so great a good that it is deservedly preferred to all physical and external goods, I said:

Now I think you see that it lies in the power of our own will to enjoy or else to lack such a great and true good. For what lies more truly in the power of the will than the will itself? [3]

In another place I wrote:

What, therefore, if the cause of our doubting (even if we never have been wise before) that it is by will that we deserve and live a praiseworthy and happy life, and by will that we deserve and live a disgraceful and unhappy life? [4]

Likewise in another place I say:

From this it is established that whoever wants to live rightly and honorably, if his will for this surpasses his will for temporal goods, achieves this great good so easily that to have what he wills is nothing other than the act of willing. [5]

Again, I said elsewhere:

The eternal law, to which it is time now to turn our attention, established with immutable firmness the point that merit lies in the will, while happiness and unhappiness are a matter of reward and punishment. [6]

In yet another place:

We have established . . . that what each man chooses to pursue and to love lies in his own will. . . . [7]

In the second book I said:

For man himself, insofar as he is a man, is a good, because he can live rightly when he so wills. [8]

[3] P. 24, § 86.
[4] P. 27, § 96.
[5] P. 28, § 97.
[6] P. 29, § 101.
[7] P. 33, § 114.
[8] P. 36, § 4.

In another passage I said that " . . . no righteous act could be performed except by free choice of the will." [9]

In the third book, I say:

Why do we have to inquire into the origin of this movement by which the will is turned from immutable to transitory goods, when we admit that it belongs to the spirit alone, and that it is voluntary and therefore blameworthy? All useful teaching on this point has its value in the fact that when this movement is disapproved and controlled, we may turn our will away from the inclination toward temporal things, to the enjoyment of eternal good.[10]

And in another place I say:

How clearly truth cries out from you! For you could not maintain that anything is in our power except actions that are subject to our own will. Therefore, nothing is so completely in our power as the will itself, for it is ready at hand to act immediately, as soon as we will.[11]

Likewise in another passage I say:

You are praised for seeing what you ought to do, even though you see this only through God, Who is immutable Truth; how much more, then, should God be praised, since He has taught you to will, has given you the power to will, and has not allowed unwillingness to go unpunished! If every man owes what he has received, and if man was made so that he must necessarily sin, then he is obliged to sin. Therefore, when he sins, he does what he ought. But if it is wicked to say this, then no one is forced to sin by his own nature.[12]

And again:

After all, what cause of the will could there be, except the will itself? It is either the will itself, and it is not possible to go back to the root of the will; or else it is not the

[9] P. 78, § 179.
[10] Pp. 87–88, § 11.
[11] P. 92, § 27.
[12] P. 124, §§ 156–57.

will, and there is no sin. Either the will is the first cause of
sin, or else there is no first cause. Sin cannot rightly be
imputed to anyone but the sinner, nor can it rightly be
imputed to him unless he wills it.[13]

And a little afterwards I say:

> For who commits sin when he cannot defend himself
> against it? But men do sin; therefore, sin can be avoided.[14]

Pelagius used these statements of mine as evidence in one of
his books. When I answered him, I entitled the book *On
Nature and Grace* [*De natura et gratia*].

In these and similar statements which I made, I did not   4
allude explicitly to the grace of God, since this was not the
subject of the inquiry; thus the Pelagians suppose, or may
suppose, that I was in agreement with their views. But they
think this in vain. As I argued in these passages, it is the will
through which we sin or live rightly. Unless the will is freed
by the grace of God from the bondage through which it has
become a slave of sin, and unless it obtains aid in conquering
its vices, mortal men cannot live rightly and piously. If this
divine gift of freedom had not preceded grace, then it would
have been given according to the merits of the will, not
through Grace, which is freely given. I have satisfactorily considered this issue in other shorter works, where I have refuted these recent heretics who deny the Doctrine of Grace.
But even in the treatise *On Free Choice of the Will*—although
it was not composed in opposition to the Pelagians at all, but
against the Manichees—I did not completely neglect God's
grace, as the former with inexpressible wickedness try to claim.
As I said in the second book:

> Not only the great goods but also the least ones can be
> from no one other than Him from whom all goods proceed,
> namely from God.[15]

[13] P. 126, §§ 168–69.
[14] P. 127, § 171.
[15] P. 80, § 191.

Again a little later:

> Therefore the virtues, by which men live rightly, are great goods, while all kinds of physical beauty [*species*], without which men can live rightly, are the lowest goods. The powers of the spirit, without which no one can live rightly, are the intermediate goods [*media bona*] between these two. No one uses the virtues for evil. However the other goods, the lowest and the intermediate ones, can be used not only for good, but also for evil. No one uses virtues for evil because the very action of a virtue is the good use of those things that we can also use for evil. Moreover, no one can make wrong use of using a thing rightly. Therefore, the abundant generosity of God's goodness is responsible not only for the great goods, but for the intermediate and lowest goods as well. His goodness ought to be praised more in the case of the greatest goods than in that of the intermediate ones, and more in the case of the intermediate goods than the lowest; but more in all goods than if He had not bestowed all.[16]

Elsewhere I say:

> Only hold to your firm faith, since no good thing comes to your perception, understanding, or thought which is not from God.[17]

Likewise, in another passage I said:

> Since a man cannot rise of his own will as he fell by his own will, let us hold with firm faith the right hand of God, Jesus Christ our Lord, which is stretched out to us.[18]

5   In the third book, after I had spoken the words which, as I mentioned, Pelagius quoted from my works—"For who commits sin when he cannot defend himself against it? But men do sin; therefore, sin can be avoided" [19]—I immediately added next:

> Yet even certain things done in ignorance are blamed and judged to need correction, as we read in the Holy Scrip-

16 Pp. 80–81, §§ 191–92.
17 P. 83, § 202.
18 P. 84, § 205.
19 P. 127, § 171.

tures where the Apostle says, "I obtained mercy because
I acted in ignorance," [20] and the prophet, "Remember
not the deeds of my youth and ignorance." There are acts
done by necessity that are to be blamed where the man
willed to act rightly and could not. For whence are these
words, . . . "To will is present with me; to accomplish that
which is good I find not." And this, "For the flesh lusts
against the spirit and the spirit against the flesh. For these
things are contrary to one another, so that you do not the
things you will." But all these things are characteristic of
men who have come from the damnation of death; for if it
is not the punishment of man, but his nature, then these
things are not sins. If a man does not depart from the
way he was made by nature—and the order of the universe
cannot be improved on—he does what he ought when he
does these things. If man were good, he would be other than
as he is. Now, however, since he is as he is, he is not good, and
does not have it in his power to be good—either because he
does not see what he ought to be, or because he does see, yet
does not have the power to be what he sees he ought to be.
Who would doubt that this is a punishment? Every penalty
that is just is a penalty for sin and is called punishment. If,
however, it is an unjust penalty, since no one doubts that
it is a penalty, it is imposed on man by some unjust ruler.
Since only a madman would doubt the omnipotence or
justice of God, the penalty is just and is a penalty for some
sin. For no unjust ruler could steal man away from God
without God's knowledge, or wrest him away against God's
will (as if God were too weak, or could be terrified or frightened!) in order to torture man with an unjust penalty. It
follows, therefore, that this just penalty comes from man's
condemnation.[21]

And elsewhere I say:

The approval of false things as true, so that man makes a
wrong judgment against his will, and the lack of power to
abstain from lust because of the opposition and torments
of the bondage of the flesh—these two things are not in the
nature of man as he was made, but are the penalties of man
who has been condemned. When we speak of the will that

[20] Scriptural attributions throughout this passage will be found on
p. 127, in the notes.
[21] Pp. 127–28, §§ 172–76.

is free to do right, we speak of the will with which man was [first] made.[22]

6   Behold! Long before the Pelagian heresy existed, we disputed as if against the Pelagians! For while goods—that is, the great, the intermediate, and the lowest—are said to be from God, free choice of the will is found to be among the intermediate goods, since we can use it for evil while yet it is such that we cannot live rightly without it. Its good use is a virtue found among the great goods, which no one can use for evil. Since, as we have said, all goods—whether great, intermediate, or lowest—are from God, it follows that the good use of free will, which is a virtue and is numbered among the great goods, is also from God. Then I proceeded to speak of the wretchedness most justly inflicted upon sinners, from which they can be freed only by God's grace; since man could fall by will, that is by free choice, he could not rise again. To the wretchedness of a just condemnation belong the ignorance and difficulty from which every man suffers from birth. No man can be freed from this evil except by the grace of God. By denying original sin, the Pelagians refuse to account for this wretchedness that results from man's just condemnation. Even though ignorance and difficulty are ingredients in man's original nature, we ought not to blame God; we ought to praise Him. This we argued in the third book. There, the discussion is directed against the Manichees, who do not acknowledge the sacred writings of the Old Testament which tell the story of original sin, and who wickedly and insolently maintain that what we read about original sin in the letters of the Apostles has been inserted as a forgery, and was not written by the Apostles at all. Yet against the Pelagians, who claim to accept them, we must defend both the Old Testament and the New.

The work *On Free Choice of the Will* begins with the words, "Tell me, please, whether God is not the cause of evil."

[22] P. 128, § 179.

INDEX

Adam, xviii; and Eve, 129. *See also* Man, first
Adultery, 6–8, 32
Africa, ix, x, xiv, 152
Ambrose, ix, xxiv
Angels, 110, 111, 112, 113, 114–15, 146
Anima, 16n
Animalia, 16
Animals. *See* Beasts
Animus, 16n
Apostles, 7
Aristotle, *Protrepticus* of, xi
Augustine: birth, x; composition of *De libero arbitrio voluntatis*, ix, xxiv, 151–52; conversion to Christianity, ix, xiii–xiv, xxiv; conversion to Manichaeism, xiv–xvi, xxii–xxiii; death, 151; education, x–xii; impression of Christ upon, xiii–xiv; negative presentation of arguments, v; style of, v, xxvi
Authority: belief through, 35, 104. *See also* Scripture
Avarice, 126
Aversio, 83

Beasts: lack of reason in, 15–17, 48–49; lack of understanding in, 40–41; sufferings of, 141–42. *See also* Man
Beauty, 74, 80
Belief, relation to understanding, 5–6, 39
Bible. *See* Scripture; *for biblical citations see* New Testament; Old Testament

Cadunt, 89
Carneades, xxiii
Carthage, x–xii, xxiii, xxiv
Casibus, 89

Chastity, 11, 12
Children: baptism of, 140; death and sufferings of, 139–41; judgments made by, 100
Christ, xii, xiv, xxii, 7, 39, 71, 84, 110, 140, 141, 148, 156; as Bread of angels, 111; as Just One, 112; as Power of God, 6; as Son of God, 6, 112; as Wisdom of God, 6; as Word of God, 111, 112
Church, Catholic, x, xxiv, xxvi
Cicero, Marcus Tullius, v, xi, xii, xiii, xiv
Communis utilitas, 13
Conversio, 83
Corinthians, I, cited, 110, 120
Corruption, 116–17, 119–20. *See also* Imperfection
Courage, 80, 82. *See also* Fortitude
Culpa, 120
Cupiditas, 8, 20

Defectivus motus, 84
Defectus, 84
De libero arbitrio voluntatis. *See* Augustine
De natura et gratia, 155
De ordine, xxvii
Desire, distinct from lust, 8–10; mind's rule over, 20
Devil, 110–13, 132–33, 146–47
Difficulty. *See* Ignorance
Discere, 4
Disciplina, 4
Divinae rationes, 97

Ecclesiastes, cited, 57
Ecclesiasticus, cited, 147
Eden, Garden of, 146
Education, 3–5; of Augustine, x–xii
Ephesians, cited, 130
Ephesus, Council of, 151

159

The Library of Liberal Arts

LEIBNIZ, G., Monadology and
Other Philosophical
Essays

LESSING, G., Laocoön

LOCKE, J., A Letter Concerning
Toleration
Second Treatise of
Government

LONGINUS, On Great Writing
(On the Sublime)

LUCIAN, Selected Works

LUCRETIUS, On Nature

MACHIAVELLI, N., The Art of War
Mandragola

MARCUS AURELIUS, Meditations

MEAD, G., Selected Writings

MILL, J., An Essay on Government

MILL, J. S., Autobiography
Considerations on
Representative
Government
Nature *and* Utility of Religion
On Liberty
On the Logic of the Moral
Sciences
Theism
Utilitarianism

MOLIÈRE, Tartuffe

MONTESQUIEU, C., The Persian
Letters

NIETZSCHE, F., The Use and Abuse
of History

NOVALIS, Hymns to the Night and
Other Writings

OCKHAM, W., Philosophical
Writings

PAINE, T., The Age of Reason

PALEY, W., Natural Theology

PARKINSON, T., ed., Masterworks
of Prose

PICO DELLA MIRANDOLA, On the
Dignity of Man, On
Being and the One, *and*
Heptaplus

PLATO, Epistles
Euthydemus
Euthyphro, Apology, Crito
Gorgias
Meno
Phaedo
Phaedrus
Protagoras
Statesman
Symposium
Theaetetus
Timaeus

Commentaries:
BLUCK, R., Plato's
Phaedo
CORNFORD, F., Plato and
Parmenides
Plato's Cosmology
Plato's Theory of
Knowledge
HACKFORTH, R., Plato's
Examination of
Pleasure
Plato's Phaedo
Plato's Phaedrus

PLAUTUS, The Haunted House
The Menaechmi
The Rope

POPE, A., An Essay on Man

POST, C., ed., Significant Cases in
British Constitutional
Law

QUINTILIAN, On the Early
Education of the
Citizen-Orator

REYNOLDS, J., Discourses on Art

Roman Drama, Copley and Hadas,
trans.

ROSENMEYER, OSTWALD, and
HALPORN, The Meters of
Greek and Latin Poetry

RUSSELL, B., Philosophy of Science

Sappho, The Poems of